Blatchford Memorial II

A Genealogical Record of the Family of
Rev. Samuel Blatchford, D. D.
With Some Mention of Allied Families

COMPILED BY

Eliphalet Wickes Blatchford

ALSO
AUTOBIOGRAPHICAL SKETCH OF
REV. DR. BLATCHFORD
FROM
"THE BLATCHFORD MEMORIAL."

The mercy of the Lord is from everlasting to everlasting upon them that fear Him, and His righteousness unto children's children; to such as keep His covenant, and to those that remember His precepts to do them.—Psalms 108:17, 18.

"He who careth not from whence he came,
careth little whither he goeth."—Daniel Webster.

PRIVATELY PRINTED
1912.

LIST OF ILLUSTRATIONS

FOREWORD

It is now forty years since the publication of "The Blatchford Memorial"—February, 1871. This book was a gift to the family from our cousin, Hon. Samuel Blatchford, LL. D., Associate Justice of the United States Supreme Court, the work being accomplished through the "assiduity and care of our cousin, Miss Harriet W. Blatchford of Troy, New York," as acknowledged in its introductory note. That volume contains the autobiographical sketch of our grandfather, Samuel Blatchford, dictated in the closing weeks of his life to his devoted daughter Jane, who acted as his amanuensis, and includes his forty-fourth year. The remaining years of his life (he died at sixty-one) are recorded by his son, our uncle, Thomas W. Blatchford, of Troy, New York. In this "Blatchford Memorial" the genealogy of the family is brought down to the date of its issue, 1871. Since that time more than a generation has passed. The Blatchford family with its more immediate connections has extended across the continent, and embraces homes beyond the Atlantic, and on the Pacific. Members of my own family have long urged that I bring this genealogy down to date, in which request others of the relatives have united. With other constant claims upon me, the securing of accurate statistics from the widely scattered membership has taken longer than I had thought when the work was begun.

Having had from an early age an interest in the family history, on my first visit to England in 1880, I engaged the services of the eminent genealogist, Sir Lemuel C. Chester, of London, to make a thorough scientific investigation of the English records of the family. This he accomplished in 1880 and '81, sending me the results with various certified documents, wills, etc., which are now in my possession. To these researches we are indebted for the carrying of the Blatchford

8

lineage one generation farther back than in the "Blatchford Memorial," and also for the verification of dates, places, facts, together with the correction of a few traditional inaccuracies. The autobiography of our grandfather, priceless to his descendants, I have incorporated in this record, omitting from it the above mentioned discrepancies. Hence it seems not inappropriate that the name of the earlier volume should be preserved in this Record, which I have, therefore, designated "BLATCHFORD MEMORIAL II."

I have added likenesses of our grandparents, and of the members of the fourth generation, these with their autographs so far as obtainable are placed near to their respective genealogies. In the fifth generation I have added the likenesses of Hon. Samuel Blatchford, LL. D., Associate Justice of the United States Supreme Court; and, at the urgent request of my children, that of the compiler of this record. I present also views of the Lansingburgh home, and the old Lansingburgh Presbyterian church.

There are also three appendices.

In Appendix "A" are presented facts concerning the Heath family,—grandfather's mother's family, so far as obtainable by Col. Chester.

Appendix "B" presents the pedigree of the Windeatt family, grandmother's line from Oliver Windeatt, A. D. 1643. Here we find the name of her grandfather, Samuel Windeatt, who, in 1729, married Sarah Edgecumbe, of Edgecumbe, and who, by his will, made generous provision for our grandmother's education. Through the kindness of our relative, Edward Windeatt, Esq., of Totnes, I am in possession of a likeness of this noble ancestor of ours—a photograph from an oil painting—which I am happy to include in this record. I also feel justified in adding to this Memorial extracts from his last will, a certified copy of which, secured by Col. Chester, lies before me. The document clearly indicates the character of the man, and his special love for his granddaughter Alice Windeatt—our grandmother. This pedigree also includes descendants of the Windeatt family still residing in Devonshire, and occupying positions of influence, who, through frequent meetings have become valued friends.

In Appendix "C" I have given records of the Hubbard

family as linked to our own through the marriage of Mrs. Henry Blatchford to Hon. Samuel Hubbard of Boston.

I would express my grateful acknowledgment to all members of the family who have aided me in securing the accuracy of this record, and trust the work may prove of interest to those for whom it was undertaken, as it has not been without its compensation to myself.

ELIPHALET WICKES BLATCHFORD,

May thirty-first, A. D. 1912,

My eighty-sixth birthday.

ULMENHEIM, 1111 LaSalle Avenue, Chicago, Illinois.

AUTOBIOGRAPHICAL SKETCH OF
THE REVEREND SAMUEL BLATCHFORD, D. D.

———

The Reverend Dr. Blatchford, in compliance with the request of his children, dictated, shortly before his death, this narrative of the principal events of his life. It comes down, however, only to the year 1807. It is addressed to his children.

I was born in the year 1767, in the town of Plymouth Dock, now called Devonport, in the county of Devon, England. My father was Henry Blatchford. My mother's name was Mary. She was the daughter of Robert Heath, of Totnes, in Devonshire.* My father was twice married. By his first wife he had a son called John, who was eminent for his piety, and died a few years since, in the triumph of faith. By his second wife, my mother, to whom he was married in the year 1766, he had four children—Samuel, Jane, Joseph, and William. William died in infancy. Joseph died at the age of five years, exhibiting a most remarkable instance of

———

* A "Silver Quart" is a relic in the family. The date on the handle is 1749. Above it are the letters " $\frac{H.}{R.M.}$ " Mrs. Alicia Blatchford, on her death bed, gave this "Silver Quart" to her oldest living son, Thomas Windeatt. In 1847, at the request of the family, the following inscription was engraved on it: "Mary, daughter of Robert and Mary Heath, wife of Henry Blatchford, and mother of the Rev. Samuel Blatchford, D. D., was born at Plymouth Dock, England, 1735." On the reverse side is the following:

"Robert Heath, of Totnes,
Mary Heath,	born 1735.
Samuel Blatchford,	" 1767.
Thomas Windeatt Blatchford,	" 1794.
Samuel T. Blatchford,	" 1822.
Thomas Windeatt Blatchford,	" 1857.
Eliphalet Wickes Blatchford,	" 1826."

he having purchased the cup August 15, 1906.

early piety, perhaps equal to any detailed in "Janeway's Token for Children." He expired in his father's arms, and spent his last laboring breath in singing the pilgrim's song —"Guide me, Oh, Thou Great Jehovah," etc. My father and mother were each of them eminent for piety. The former owed his first religious impressions to the preaching of the Reverend John Wesley, and the latter to that of the venerable Rowland Hill.

Having been early devoted by my parents to the service of the sanctuary, should it please God to make me a subject of divine grace, my studies were directed with a special reference to that object. My English education was superintended by a Mr. Waters, whose name I cannot mention but with the greatest respect, on account of that faithful and pious discharge of his duty toward me which has been a source of benefit I can never forget. My classical studies commenced at an early age, first under the care of the Reverend Mr. King, and afterward under the Reverend Mr. Stokes, both of whom were clergymen in the Episcopal Church, and were considered men of science.

About this time the American Revolution commenced, an event which excited the interest of all Europe, and brought forward, even in England, many open friends to the claims of America, and the rights and liberty of the Provinces. Among these were my relatives, who distinguished themselves, as Providence gave them opportunity, by manifesting the sincerity of their zeal. This was particularly the case with the Reverend Robert Heath, my mother's eldest brother, who, together with my mother, essentially ameliorated the sufferings of the American prisoners who were confined in Mill Prison at Dartmoor. From their own resources they advanced considerable sums, until, at length, a benevolent association was formed in London, for this purpose. On referring to a letter which I received from my uncle Heath, dated February 13th, 1797, I find that the Marquis of Rockingham, the Duke of Richmond, and several other conspicuous characters, were at the head of this noble institution. "It was at the request of these noblemen," says Mr. Heath, "who formed the committee of this society, that I undertook to distribute such subscriptions as might be raised for this purpose of benevolence. That which I was privileged in doing afforded me sincere pleasure, for, they were in a state in which they could not help themselves." The assistance was sometimes conveyed by Mr. Heath's direct agency, and sometimes I was employed, as being less subject to suspicion. In consequence of this, I was compelled to spend portions of several days in each week in that prison where our American brethren were treated rather as rebels against the government than as prisoners of war. The kindness with which I was received by these poor fellows, and the frequent conversations which I held with them relative to their country and their homes, awakened within me feelings by no means transient, and led me, at that early age, to determine that, when I became a man, I would choose my residence in America. I well remember their expressions of gratitude; and their sincerity was testified by the numerous little presents which I constantly received from them, consisting of carved boxes, box inkstands, and miniature ships, beautifully rigged.

The spiritual wants of these poor fellows were not neglected. Bibles and hymn books were distributed among them, and Mr. Heath would frequently address them on the subject of religion. Nor did the charities of these benevolent individuals stop here. Retreats were provided for such as fortunately should make their escape. Among these happy few, was the late Captain Smedley, collector of customs at the port of Fairfield, in Connecticut. He was concealed in the house of a Mrs. Chenough, whither I have often been sent with means of relief for him and others.

Before an opportunity arose for forwarding those concealed at Mrs. Chenough's to Holland, on their way to America, the following circumstance occurred: A gentleman, captain of a vessel of war, but whose name I do not recollect, had been secreted at my father's until the search after him was supposed to be over. To effect his return, it was determined that he should accompany my uncle and my mother to London. A post-chaise received them about three o'clock in the morning, and they travelled unmolested as far as Holdon Heath, an extensive Common of flinty soil, between Plymouth Dock and Exeter, when, hearing the trampling of horses, my uncle perceived, from the glass in the back of the chaise, that a company of horsemen was pursuing them. In this extremity, the expedient was adopted, of placing the fugitive on the bottom of the carriage, and concealing him with their cloaks. The company, having overtaken them, caused the postillion to stop. Observation was made by the officer, and the company passed on, after having made an apology for detaining them. They now hoped to meet with no further molestation, but soon perceived that the horsemen had halted, and were waiting the coming up of the carriage. The postillion was again ordered to stop, the former process was repeated, and they then passed on towards the city. Whether the fugitive was really being pursued or not, could not be ascertained. My uncle thought it prudent, instead of going into the city, to enter the lower suburbs, and proceed immediately to the town of Collumpton, about twelve miles distant, on the Bristol road. At Collumpton they changed carriages, and reached London in safety. My mother, who was a woman of timid make, although not apprehensive at the time of suffering any evil effects from her fright, underwent, in consequence of it, a severe attack of illness. She was removed from the carriage to her bed at her brother's, Mr. Richard Heath's, and was unable to leave it for the space of six weeks.

When I was between the ages of seven and nine years, I experienced two instances of divine interference in the preservation of life, when exposed to imminent danger. The first of these was the following: I had been amusing myself nearly the whole of an afternoon by fishing from a boat which lay beside the dock, and was so much occupied by my employment, that I did not perceive the falling of the tide. It fell, I think, about twelve or fourteen feet. It now became a question how to return, and I determined to clamber up by the help of the projecting stones by which the pier was built. In the attempt, one of the stones gave way, and I fell between the boat and the pier. At the adjoining pier lay a collier, of about three hundred tons burden, on the yard-arm of which was a Mr. Blewits, belonging to the Customs. He swung off from the yards by means of a rope, and caught me by my hair, and thus rescued me from a watery grave.

The second circumstance, to which I have referred, was this: I was requested to ride my uncle's horse from Stoke, his country residence, to Plymouth Dock. As I approached the drawbridge which covered the foss, (for Plymouth Dock was a fortified town,) I slid, by some means, from the saddle, and my left leg caught in the stirrup. No one was near to render me assistance, excepting the sentry, who was on guard at the time; and he could not leave his post without a breach of orders, which would subject him to punishment. But the invisible God was present, and graciously sustained me until the horse drew me, without injury, within the limits beyond which the sentry could not pass. "Whoso is wise, and will observe these things, even they shall understand the loving-kindness of the Lord."

The first religious impressions which I recollect, (although a tenderness of conscience was remarkably preserved, through the influence of that pious care which was taken of my earliest youth,) commenced when I was between eight and nine years of age, under a sermon by the Reverend Andrew Kinsmans, from the words, "The Master is come, and calleth for thee." I then felt myself to be a sinner, and altogether unfit to appear in the Master's presence, as he stood in the character of a judge, by whose righteous judgment I thought I must be eternally condemned. Although the pungency of these impressions, in a measure, wore off, yet I was still followed by exercises of a very serious nature, until about the age of twelve, when the Lord was pleased, as I humbly hope, to further, by his own spirit, the word of grace. It was under the preaching of a colleague of Mr. Kinsmans, a Mr. Dunn, from Psalm 80, verse 19, "Turn us again," etc. My distress was very great, and my affliction called forth the solicitude of my parents. My father urged upon me the great truths of the gospel, as the claim which God had upon the hearts of his creatures, the necessity of regeneration and the certainty of salvation to all who should obtain reconciliation with God through the merits of the sacrifice of Christ. These prayers and exhortations, were, I trust, instrumental in causing me to seek, and, as I trust, to obtain, a hope which will never make me ashamed. Now was I peculiarly delighted with the idea of being, at some future time, honored of God by entering the ministry. With this view, I was sent to a boarding-school, at Wellington, in Somersetshire, under the care of the

Reverend Joseph Chadwick, a dissenting clergyman of piety, and fine literary endowments. Under his care I was prepared to become a member of the dissenting college of theology, at Homerton, near London.

Previously, however, to my removal from Wellington, it pleased God to visit my dear father with a disease which terminated in his death. He was a rich partaker in the grace of God, lived much in the fellowship with the Father and with his Son Jesus Christ, and, in the sixty-third year of his age, terminated his earthly pilgrimage, and entered into that rest which remaineth for the people of God—an inheritance incorruptible, undefiled, and that fadeth not away. He was a most affectionate parent. My last interview with him I can never forget. He took me with him to Mount Batton, a favorite retreat, about half a mile from Plymouth Dock. After having spent a considerable time there, during which we experienced mingled emotions of pleasure and pain, we set out on our return. Having reached a retired field, I received his last advice, and, while we knelt down together on the sod, he renewedly dedicated me to God, and solemnly implored the blessing of a covenant God and Father to rest upon a beloved son whom he expected never again to see in this vale of tears—this land of separation.

Notwithstanding my parents had early designed me for the gospel ministry, yet, under the influence of one or two relatives, my mother was prevailed upon to think of another profession for me. Nothing had been said to me of this design, until I was introduced to Dr. Lawrence Reeves,* an eminent surgeon in the city of London, when, to my astonishment, the plan was developed. But my own mind was too intently fixed upon the gospel ministry, to accede to the proposal; so that, after having tarried two or three weeks in London, I returned to Wellington, where, having finished my course of studies, I entered, as a student, the theological seminary at Homerton, which afforded many important advantages to theological students. The professors were men eminently qualified to fill the stations they were called to occupy in that interesting school of the prophets. It has been the means of sending forth to the furtherance of Christ's

* His uncle by marriage.

glorious kingdom, many eminently useful men, who will doubtless "shine as the brightness of the firmament." The professors at that time were the Reverend Benjamin Davis, classical, oriental, and resident professor; the Reverend Daniel Fisher, D. D., professor of didactic and polemic divinity; and Dr. Thomas Gibbon, professor of belles-lettres, ecclesiastical history, etc., etc. Dr. Gibbon died during my second year, and was succeeded by the Reverend Henry May, D. D.

Dr. Gibbon is generally known in this country as the editor of President Davies' sermons, and as his particular friend. He was also the intimate and confidential friend of Dr. Isaac Watts. Many were the pleasant communications respecting Dr. Watts which Dr. Gibbons was pleased to make to the students. He was with him during his sickness and at his death, and often spoke of the firmness of his hope, breathing after immortality, and finding the precious promises of the gospel his support in a dying hour. "With the highest degree of satisfaction," said Dr. Gibbon, "did he speak of that blessed method revealed in the Holy Scriptures, whereby we may be saved, exhibiting, at once, the perfections of God and the mysteries of his grace, encouraging the helpless but convinced sinner to look for pardon and peace through the atoning blood of Jesus Christ; the great sacrifice by which God could be just and yet justify the repenting and believing sinner. His whole soul seemed to be filled with gratitude and joy for the redemption of sinners by Jesus Christ. He esteemed as nothing his labors, his accomplishments, and his merits, and gave all the glory to Him who had called him out of darkness into marvellous light and the hope of reconciliation with God. A little before he expired, to the inquiry, 'How is it with your soul?' he emphatically replied, 'All is comfortable there.' The age in which he lived might, perhaps, be styled an age of theological and philosophical speculation. Dr. Watts was not deficient in speculations on the most important points of divinity. This was his principal fault. Among other doctrines essential to the Christian system is the doctrine of the Trinity. To this he yielded implicit belief, as it is revealed in the Scriptures, and believed by the orthodox church at large." Thus far we have the testimony of Dr.

Gibbons. The speculations of Dr. Watts as to the modus of existence of the sacred three gave birth to a variety of attempts, on the part of Arians and Sabellians, to enlist his name as an authority on their side of the question. These, however, could never succeed during the life-time of Dr. Gibbons, and of others who were personally acquainted with Dr. Watts. But, after the death of Dr. Gibbons, great efforts were made by a distinguished individual, an advocate for the indwelling scheme, to accomplish this object. His design was to publish anonymously, lest the knowledge of the author should detract from the influence of the work. In this, however, he was defeated by a mistake of the printer's boy, who providentially left the proof-sheets at another house than the author's. I have never thought it strange that Arians, Sabellians, and other Anti-Christians should anxiously seek the support of the reputation of so distinguished an individual; but I have been exceedingly surprised that there should exist, among a section of the Protestant church, a disposition to urge the charge of heterodoxy against Dr. Watts, as a reason for neglecting, in their worship, the use of his invaluable psalms and hymns.

The seminary at Homerton afforded many delightful opportunities for religious exercise, which were gladly improved by many of the students. It is well known that, around London, there are several charitable establishments, intended for the accommodation of widows whose piety and poverty recommend them to the benevolence of the churches. These establishments accommodate variously from four to eight widows, each occupying a separate apartment, where they are furnished with the various comforts of life. Here they are able to hold sweet converse together, and trace the dealings of Divine Providence, with adoring conceptions of the covenant faithfulness of the widow's God. At several of these places were established weekly lectures, conducted by the theological students. It was delightful, in these little congregations, formed of the widowed mothers in Israel, to mingle in prayer and praise, and meditate on the great truths of the gospel. With them I was often permitted to meet; and often have I felt encouraged and animated by these precious saints, who seemed already to have learned the language of the heavenly

Canaan, and longed for the universal extension of the kingdom of our Lord Jesus Christ. Often have I thought, could they have looked forward to the day in which we live and marked the signs of the times which afford prospects of such a pleasing character, could they have seen the general diffusion of the word of God amongst the nations of the earth, and attended the living preacher with the Bible in his hand, publishing the mysteries of the Cross and proffering the salvation of the gospel to Jews and infidels, to idolaters and savage men, could they have known the success with which these efforts have been crowned, how would their hearts have been filled with holy joy, and the song of praise have broken from their lips, to the honor of the Lamb that was slain. But they have doubtless, long ere this, been made acquainted with these triumphs of divine grace.

During my last year at Homerton, I had an invitation to preach, during the vacation, in the town of Plymouth, in the congregation of the Reverend C. Mends and his son Herbert Mends, who were co-pastors in the same church, and also in a congregation connected with it, at Stonehouse, about a mile from Plymouth Dock. I labored about six weeks, during the absence of Mr. Herbert Mends, not I trust without success.

About this time, I was introduced to the Reverend William Evans, pastor of the united congregations of Kingsbridge and Ford, where I had occasionally preached. When I had completed my theological studies, I accepted an invitation to assist the above-named gentleman in the duties of the sanctuary. Immediately after my settlement, I entered into a matrimonial engagement with Miss Alicia Windeatt, my present wife. She was the daughter of Thomas Windeatt, of Bridgetown, Totnes. Our marriage took place on the 25th of March, 1788. This connection has ever been to me a source of happiness, for which I cannot be sufficiently thankful to Him who is the great disposer of all events.

Previously to our marriage, an invitation was presented to me, through the Reverend Dr. Lake, of London, to accompany Lord Dorchester to Canada, to the governorship of which he was appointed. The design, which was originated by Charles James Fox, was to establish, under the patronage of the British government, a Presbyterian Church, with privileges equal to those enjoyed by the Episcopal Church, in order to induce persons to emigrate from the United States to Canada. The salary offered was £300 sterling per annum, with other emoluments, and I was to be returned at the expense of the government, if dissatisfied with the situation. This offer was declined, on account of the opposition of my intended wife's friends. After this, a second proposition, of a similar nature, was made to me, but, for similar reasons as before, I again declined, and Lord Dorchester sailed without me. The design of countenancing Presbyterianism in Canada, with equal privileges with those enjoyed by Episcopalianism, has, I believe, from that time, been abandoned.

We commenced housekeeping immediately after our marriage, in the village of Ford. At this place was born our eldest son, Henry, on the 4th of December, 1788. The inhabitants were mostly farmers, whose simple manners, sincerity, and readiness to oblige, contributed much to our comfort; but, as the house in which we dwelt was about to be occupied by the owner, we removed to Frogmore, a village about half way between my two congregations at Ford and Kingsbridge. Circumstances now having arisen, which made it appear desirable to the friends of religion that I should be inducted into the pastoral office over the church and congregation in Kingsbridge, I acted accordingly. This, however, was not to interrupt the arrangement I had made with Mr. Evans, for preaching alternately at Ford and Kingsbridge. It was with a sincere desire to be instrumental in promoting the interests of the cause of Christ, and with a deep sense of responsibility, that I consented to this arrangement. My ordination took place at Kingsbridge, according to the following certificate: "Kingsbridge, November 4th, 1789. This is to certify, to all whom it may concern, that the Reverend Samuel Blatchford, who was educated at Homerton, (London,) was this day solemnly set apart to the pastoral office, over the Presbyterian church in Kingsbridge, (Devon,) with prayer and laying on of hands by us. William Evans, C. Mends, H. Mends, Jas. Stowal."

Of the Reverend Mr. Evans, my venerable and beloved colleague, I could say much. He might be portrayed as eminently pious and amiable; and greatly am I indebted to him

ALICIA WINDEATT

(From a miniature on ivory, made
before her marriage)

for the kindness which he showed to me during the earlier years of my ministry. I was with him as a child with a father; and it may please you, my children, to learn with what partiality and strong regard he ever cultivated my memory. I will, therefore, here insert a letter which I received from him in 1810. He has long since gone to his rest, and, doubtless, has received that crown of life promised unto them who are faithful unto death. He was a faithful and laborious servant of our Lord and Saviour Jesus Christ. The letter I referred to, commences thus: "Oh, my dear Blatchford, whose memory is fresh in my mind, and ever dear, we often speak of you, and scenes pleasant, scenes past, which, alas, will never be experienced again in this world. How short are the best comforts of this life! When we have our families, as olive branches, around our tables, and are placed in the midst of a circle of select and valued friends, how soon, alas, is our happiness interrupted, and we torn asunder from those whom we most regard and love, and a rent is made which can never be closed. So it shall not be in the society of the blessed in Heaven; there separation shall never take place, and joy shall never end. May our hearts be there with our best friends, and, best of all, our dear, dear Immanuel.".

The 24th of January, 1790, gave birth to our beloved daughter, Mary Milford Windeatt.

My continuance at Kingsbridge was but of short duration. Having received an invitation from the church and congregation in Topsham, near the city of Exeter, in Devonshire, I removed thither early in the year 1791. This was a long established Presbyterian Church. In it the Arian and Sabellian heresies had, for some years, prevailed. However, under all the circumstances of the case, being particularly urged by some of my orthodox brethren, whose judgment could not but be respected, and resting upon the blessing of God, and depending upon the promise of Christ, "Lo, I am with you always," etc., I entered upon the duties of so important a station.

On the 14th of February, 1791, was born Alicia Windeatt; on the 23d of April, 1792, Sarah; and, on the 3d of May, 1793, Samuel. The latter two died at an early age and full of promise. He who gave them, and who alone had the sovereign right of recalling them, was pleased to bereave us of these tender plants. Sarah died June 23d, 1793, aged fourteen months. Samuel died February 3d, 1794, aged twenty-one months. They lie buried in a vault under the communion table in the meeting-house at Topsham. These domestic sorrows were severely felt, as afflictions of Divine Providence, which, whilst calculated to try our faith, cannot be endured without bitterness, which parental fondness often mingles with an unsparing hand in the cup of trial.

> "The parent's heart,
> Doubled in wedlock, multiplied in children,
> Stands but the broader mark for all the mischiefs
> That rove promiscuous o'er this mortal stage.
> Children, those dear young lambs, those tender pieces
> Of our own flesh, those little other selves,
> How they dilate the heart to wide dimensions,
> And soften every fibre, to improve
> The parent's sad capacity for pain."

While in the midst of the enjoyment of a social visit at the house of the Reverend Mr. Meggs of the Established Church, I received a message from home, requesting my immediate return, on account of the dangerous illness of my daughter Sarah. I arrived at home in the course of the night, but only to embrace a dying child. Her funeral was appointed to take place on the Saturday following. It was attended by the Reverend* Robert Winton, a very beloved brother, who was settled at Exmouth, about six miles distant from me. Just previous to this solemnity, I received a letter from my sister, informing me that my son Henry was dangerously ill at Plymouth, and requiring my immediate presence. This news overwhelmed us with grief and consternation. Our little Samuel was at this time unbaptized, and not knowing how far the visitation of the Almighty might extend, the sacred duty of devoting him to the Lord in baptism was immediately performed. After the funeral of our beloved Sarah, the same brother who had pronounced over our departed babe the decree of the Almighty, "Dust thou art and unto dust shalt

---

* See account of Rev. Robert Winton, with his likeness, in "Congregational Sunday Schools, Chard, Somersetshire, England, Their Rise and Progress," by T. W. Sanders, 1906.

HOUSE OF SAMUEL WINDEATT,
BRIDGETOWN, TOTNES, DEVONSHIRE, ENGLAND

The home of Our Grandmother—Alicia Windeatt, up to the date of her marriage, March
25, 1788, at the age of twenty and one half years

thou return," now took the little survivor in his arms, and baptized him "in the name of the Father, and of the Son, and of the Holy Ghost." After the performance of this duty, I started for Plymouth, without delay. I was going as I supposed to the house of mourning. I arrived at my mother's about six o'clock in the evening, and, the family being engaged in another part of the house, I hastened to the room in which I knew my son was accustomed to sleep, where, to my inexpressible surprise mingled with feelings of thankfulness and gratitude to God, which His merciful interference so emphatically demanded, I found the dear child in a sweet slumber, and, as I conceived, entirely out of danger. So, indeed, the event proved. This interference of God, so timely and wonderfully displayed, completely assuaged my grief for the loss of my beloved Sarah, so that I could do little else than praise God and give thanks. The next day I was enabled to preach with that composure and tranquillity, and grateful sense of the goodness of God, which His providences were calculated to produce.

I have mentioned the Reverend Robert Winton. Of our intimacy and brotherly attachment you may form some idea from the following extract from a letter received from him shortly after my arrival in America: "Exmouth, November 30th, 1795. My very dear brother: I received your letter on the 11th inst. It is impossible for me to express the pleasure it gave me to hear that you and your dear family were all safely arrived at your destined place of residence. With flowing eyes and a feeling heart I bowed me down and returned thanks to Him to whom thanks were due. I had long been looking for a letter from you, and, ere it came, many from different parts called upon me to know if I had heard from you, and when, at last, I was able to say that I had, and that you were well, every one expressed their joy and many wished themselves with you."

On the 20th of July, 1794, we were blessed with another son, whom we called Thomas Windeatt, after his maternal grandfather.

About two years after my removal to Topsham, the subject of Sabbath schools engaged the attention of many benevolent persons. The success of Mr. Raikes, of Gloucester, in his attempt to educate the ignorant and reclaim the vicious among the poor and neglected youth, left no doubt as to the utility of such efforts. After looking around, therefore, on the population of the town where Providence had placed me, and, with the aid of some influential persons, obtaining, in some degree, a knowledge of the wretched situation in which many of the poor children lived—many of whom had never been taught to read or write, and, from year to year, had never entered a place of worship, they being during the week, chiefly occupied in picking oakum, the profits arising from which contributed in a very small degree to their support, and passing the Sabbath in acts exceedingly offensive to good morals—we determined to attempt the establishment of a Sabbath school. The friends of this measure, however, were not without apprehensions of opposition. Many of them were well known to be dissenters from the Church of England, and this was asserted to be a measure of theirs to draw away youth from the Establishment. A public meeting was called, and the opposition came out in its strength; but God overruled all for good. He made the wrath of man to praise Him, and restrained the remainder of wrath. It was urged, that the Sabbath school would produce injurious effects, by teaching children to read, but more particularly to write. The Reverend Mr. C. declared it to be as preposterous a measure, to attempt the reformation of society by the instruction of youth, as to commence building a house at the top of a chimney. These objections were easily answered, and the friends of the measure felt themselves warranted in commencing their operations. A sum of money sufficient for this purpose was soon collected, and a Sabbath school was established, with flattering prospects of success. Our plan was entirely different from the one now in successful operation in this country. Now, the instructions are administered by the voluntary aid of individuals, who, as philanthropists, desire to promote the best interests of their fellow creatures, by instilling into the minds of the ignorant those principles of virtue which will reclaim our wandering youth from ignorance and vice to intelligence and a fitting sense of their obligations, and as Christians, estimating the value of the immortal soul and the importance of the enlargement of the

BERRY POMEROY CHURCH, DEVONSHIRE, ENGLAND,
Where Rev. Samuel Blatchford and Alicia Windeatt were married

Redeemer's kingdom, would lead these youth to a knowledge of the sacred Scriptures, which reveal to man the way of salvation. But, in England, and at that time, when those institutions were in their infancy, we were under the necessity of hiring teachers at a stated salary. We opened four distinct schools—two for boys and two for girls. Thus our youth were taught the Scriptures and the Catechism, and were furnished by the hand of charity with decent clothing. I acted the part of a superintendent. My custom was to spend the intervals of worship in these schools, from eight to ten o'clock A. M. and from one to two and from six to eight P. M.; to commence with prayer; to sit while the instructors heard the lessons; then to hear the Catechism which had been committed through the week; and to close the whole with a brief exhortation, adapted, as far as was in my power, to the capacities of my youthful auditors. Great care was taken not to wound the feelings of persons of different denominations, and the scholars attended the places of worship desired by their parents. God was pleased to smile upon these labors, and I trust they were blessed to the salvation of many of the children.

About this time, my predisposition to remove to America was much strengthened, and I began to take some measures preparatory to emigrating. My wife, animated by that affection which has ever characterized her since her connection with myself, assented cheerfully to my plans. An old and faithful friend of the family, Capt. Furze, informed me that he was soon to sail for America, where he had some acquaintance, and where he intended to take up his own residence. I thought it expedient to put into his hands a list of inquiries, which I deemed of importance. At these you will probably smile. I can only find an apology in the almost necessary ignorance of an entire stranger to the habits and customs of Americans. These were as follows: "What is the salary generally offered to clergymen? Is there generally a glebe attached to places of worship? What is the price of provisions in different places? What is the price of labor? What are the wages of servants? Would a school be likely to prosper, and where? I do not care in what part of America I settle, if the climate be healthy, and I can enjoy Christian society, and be useful as a minister of the gospel. I can obtain recommendations from all the ministers in Devonshire. Please to hand this to the ministers of the places where you may be, and, though I am a stranger to them, I doubt not their readiness to give you satisfaction as to the above questions, and I trust the time will soon come when I shall greet the generous Americans on their own territory. Topsham, May 3d, 1794. S. Blatchford.''

Early in the year 1795, I received a letter from Capt. Furze, which called for the following reply, addressed to the Church of Christ, at Bedford, in Westchester county, New York: ''To the Church of Christ, at Bedford. Christian friends and brethren: Having received a letter from Capt. Furze, with the information of your being destitute of a minister, and of your desire to communicate with me on the subject of my settling among you, I feel myself bound to address you. I have long felt a desire to become an inhabitant of America, and, with a wife and four children, partake of the blessings of a country distinguished for its general piety, the excellence of its government, and the free exercise of religious opinions. Unlike to England, the principles of conscience are not overawed by a bigoted clergy, but every Christian Society can fully enjoy that liberty wherewith Christ has made them free. I have often considered the decay of religion as keeping pace with the extension of ecclesiastical authority, and, surely, infidelity and profaneness never ran in a wider channel, never rushed in a more impetuous torrent, than at present; never was religion more controverted, never was it less practised. Mankind, to avoid preciseness, have fallen into licentiousness, and, through an aversion to mysteries, have run away from godliness. I should have embarked last spring, but did not wish to go on a plan altogether uncertain. It may be necessary to say, that my religious principles are Calvinistic, and that I have been engaged in the ministry about eight years, have been ordained five, and was educated at the Dissenting College, at Homerton, near London. Let me desire you, as soon as convenient, to answer the above. In expectation of which, I remain your friend and brother in the Gospel, S. Blatchford.'' To this letter I received an answer from Dr. Fleming and Deacon Taylor, expressing an ardent desire that I should visit them as soon as possible. After seeking direc-

1768

March 25th

No. Then was Married Mr. Samuel Blatchford of Thurlaston

Occupation Minister & Miss Ann Wisvdead of Berry Pomeroy

I hereby certify that the above is a true Copy of the Entry made in the Marriage Register Book of the Parish of Berry-Pomeroy, in the County of Devon, and extracted this ___21st___ day of ___October___ in the year of our Lord, one thousand eight hundred and ___Seventy-Five___

by me _____ Vicar

tion from the Father of Lights, we were led to the conclusion
that it was our duty to remove. We accordingly took measures for the accomplishment of our design. I determined
therefore, to make my congregation acquainted with my purpose. After mature deliberation, they reluctantly assented to
a separation. There is a tie which unites a pastor to his people, which cannot be sundered without feelings of regret.
Letters were at this time written to London, relative to a passage to New York. We received an answer that there was a
vessel bound for that port, but her time of sailing was uncertain. The price of passage was forty guineas per head for
adults, and half that amount for children and servants, together with freight for baggage, according to admeasurement.
On account of the extravagance of these terms, and of the
distance from Topsham to London, as well as the uncertainty
of the time when the vessel would sail, we were obliged to seek
some other conveyance. It was then hoped that a passage
might be obtained on more reasonable terms at Bristol, but
we were again disappointed. We had, at the suggestion of
Capt. Furze, laid out considerable property in goods, which,
he informed us, might be sold to considerable advantage in
America, and he kindly offered to furnish us with what specie
we wanted on our arrival. It was, and had been for many
years, a maxim by which I had been governed, that if Almighty God had designed us to fill any particular station,
His Divine Providence would open the way. So it was in
this case. About three or four weeks previously to this time,
a vessel sustained considerable injury at no great distance
from the port of Topsham, and was brought in thither in
order to undergo repairs. It was given out that she was
bound to America, and I accordingly communicated with the
captain, whose name was Lyon, relative to my sailing with
him. His terms were, however, higher than those proffered
either in London or Bristol, which occasioned much hesita-
tion in my mind about accepting them; and, indeed, I was
doubtful whether to undertake the voyage at all. But I had
gone so far as to obtain the consent of my wife's family and of
my congregation, and had given notice of my intention to
preach my farewell sermon on a particular day, and I was
unable to determine how to act. I was led, however, to seek

the direction of my Heavenly Father, and with fervency to
pray that He who was a cloud by day and a pillar of fire by
night to his ancient Israel, would condescend to be my guide,
and that, if it was His will that I should leave my native
shores for a strange land, He would be graciously pleased to
direct me in the pursuit of my object. The Sabbath at length
arrived on which I was to take leave of the people of my
charge. The place of worship was crowded, and a scene of
peculiar interest was presented by the children of the Sabbath schools, all of whom attended on the occasion. My text
was found in 2 Corinthians, chapter 5, verses 9 and 10:
"Wherefore we labor, that, whether present or absent, we may
be accepted of Him. For, we must all appear before the
judgment seat of Christ." My own feelings on this occasion
may be better imagined than described. A weeping audience
—a collection of about two hundred children—a separation
about to take place from those to whom I had preached for
five years, and from children whom I had been instrumental
in gathering from the highways and hedges, whose temporal
and eternal welfare I ardently desired and sedulously endeavored to ensure—awakened within me feelings to which I had
before been a stranger. It was with difficulty I could leave
the place of worship, owing to the anxiety of friends to express their sentiments of affectionate regard. In the avenue
which led from the church to the street, I found the children
of the Sabbath school, many of them weeping aloud, and all
desirous of expressing their sorrow at the separation about to
take place. Several of my friends accompanied me to my
dwelling-house, where, we were soon surprised by the sound
of the voices of the Sabbath school children, who, in front of
the house, were singing the following hymn:

> "Blest be the charity divine,
>   Which tends to form the infant mind,
>   Which puts the youth in virtue's road,
>   And points the path that leads to God.
>
> Erewhile, in ignorance we lay,
>   Of folly and of vice the prey,
>   Not knowing what we ought to do,
>   How evil shun or good pursue.

> Now taught to know God's holy will,
> His just commands may we fulfil,
> His Sabbath keep, his name adore,
> His goodness love, and fear his power.
>
> Blest be the charity divine
> That thus instructs the tender mind,
> Places the youth in virtue's road
> And leads him on the way to God.''

The whole company was deeply affected. As yet no light was shed on my future path; but God soon manifested himself to be a present help in time of need. In the evening I received a message from Capt. Lyon, requesting that I would call and see him immediately on business of importance. I returned an answer, that I attended to no business on the Sabbath, except such as was connected with its sacred duties. The messenger soon returned with an answer, that, from the nature of the business, there could be no impropriety in my complying with Capt. Lyon's request. I accordingly called upon him, and found that his mind had been seriously impressed by the exercises of the day. ''Your first sentence,'' said he, ''after you pronounced your text, produced an indescribable effect upon my mind.'' He immediately, even with tears, expressed his desire to convey me and my family to America on any terms. Truly I had reason to say:

> ''God moves in a mysterious way,
> His wonders to perform.''

It is impossible to describe the sensations which I experienced at this interposition of Divine Providence, which so unexpectedly rendered our plans feasible, and so wonderfully spoke a language which could not be misunderstood. It seemed to say—take courage and go forward. The proposal of Capt. Lyon could not be thought of without gratitude to God, who had disposed his mind to an act so truly generous. On my return home, having communicated the circumstance to my wife, we both, feeling the faithfulness of Him of whom it is said, ''In all thy ways acknowledge Him, and He shall direct thy paths,'' immediately called the family together, when, kneeling down before the throne of Divine Grace, we endeavored humbly to acknowledge the goodness of God, and to commit ourselves renewedly to his watchful care and merciful Providence.

Capt. Lyon was anxious to convey me and my family to America without receiving any remuneration, but, as I could not consent to this, he requested me to name the price of passage. As I would not consent to this, he proposed twenty guineas for myself and the same amount for Mrs. B. As for the children, who were four in number, he said that he would adopt them as his own during the voyage, and, of course, would charge nothing for the servant, as she was necessary to take care of the children. His vessel, he said, was large enough to carry all my baggage, and he would make no charge for that. At the sale of my furniture, Capt. Lyon bought to the amount of the price of our passage, and distributed the articles he purchased among his friends at Totnes. A Sabbath intervening between the time of which I have been speaking and our embarkation, we concluded to spend it at Exmouth, about six miles from Totnes. Here I preached twice, and was gratified by the presence of several members of my late congregation.

On the 19th of June, 1795, we left our native shores, and committed ourselves to the guardian care of Him whom the winds and the seas obey. A large crowd of people assembled on the hill which overlooked the sea, and long continued, by the waving of hats and handkerchiefs, to manifest the affectionate interest which they took in our departure. As we receded, objects on the shore became less and less distinct, until lost in the distance. During the voyage my influence over the captain and crew constantly increased, and, on the Sabbath, I used regularly to preach to them on deck. We enjoyed a good degree of health, excepting that I had a slight attack of inflammation in the face, and my wife received a severe wound from the falling of my portable desk. We suffered considerably from want of water, when about opposite Newfoundland, and had just concluded to steer thither, when we were unexpectedly favored with a shower of rain, and, by means of the sails, we caught enough to supply our wants. At length, on the 1st day of August, 1795, the day on which I completed my twenty-eighth year, we arrived within the Hook, at New York. The night was dark, and the captain had concluded to anchor outside the Hook, and wait for a pilot, but, before he was aware, found himself abreast of Staten Island, having securely, but unintentionally, passed in without a pilot.*

With my wife and family, I immediately went on shore, accompanied by Capt. Lyon, and, having left my family at the City Hotel, at that time in Water street, I set out in search of Capt. Furze, who had given me his address, at Mr. William Sing's, hardware merchant, whose store was in Hanover Square. Mr. Sing was at his house in Brooklyn, but I saw a young man of pleasing appearance, who expressed himself much gratified at my arrival. I was much disappointed to learn that Capt. Furze, on whom I depended both for resources and direction, had left the city two days previously, for Albany, and that his return was very uncertain. For my present accommodation, however, I had been recommended for lodgings, by Capt. Furze, to the house of Mrs. Stynetz, in Barclay street, at the corner nearly opposite the Roman Catholic chapel. The young gentleman above mentioned, together with Mr. Sing, belonged to the Baptist denomination. I was introduced by them to the Reverend Dr. Rodgers, of the University of Pennsylvania, who at that time was on a visit to New York and was officiating that day in the duties of the Sanctuary. He kindly bid me welcome, and urged me to preach for him, but I declined. I consented, however, to assist him in the devotional exercises of the evening; and this I was enabled to do with a feeling sense of God's goodness, in the preservation of myself and my dear family, during a voyage which lasted forty-three days. My feelings overwhelmed me, and the sensibility of the audience awakened a sympathy which I cannot describe. Several of them called the next day at Mr. Sing's store, in hopes of seeing me, in order to proffer their services in enabling me to reach the place of my destination—Bedford. Mr. Sing accompanied me to the Custom House, where the duties I had to pay nearly exhausted my

* The vessel—the schooner Alert—was lost on her return voyage and all hands perished.

finances. I was, however, amply supplied with money by a
providential circumstance. As I was walking down Wall
street, I was accosted by R. A. Haim, Esq., who had lately
arrived from Totnes, having married a young lady of that
town. After some conversation respecting my voyage, he
asked how I was off for money. He then desired me to name
the sum of money I wanted, and, agreeably to my request,
lent me one hundred dollars. Thus supplied, and with the
advice of Mr. Sing, I engaged passage for myself and family
to Sing Sing, about thirty miles up the Hudson, and about
twelve distant from Bedford. We arrived safely in the afternoon, and, after my baggage was landed and my family safely
lodged at a tavern, I started in pursuit of a Capt. Hunter,
who had been recommended as being able to render me such
services as might be necessary for my accommodation. The
regret which I felt at the absence of Capt. Furze produced a
perplexity and a dejection which I could scarcely overcome.
But God was still on my side. As I was walking toward
Capt. Hunter's house, I heard a voice distinctly pronounce
my name, and, looking in the direction from whence the voice
came, I saw Capt. Furze. He had returned from Albany the
evening before, not having been able to accomplish his business there. This was truly a remarkable Providence. It
relieved my embarrassment and soothed my feelings. I immediately returned to the tavern, accompanied by Capt. Furze,
and had the pleasure of introducing him to your dear mother,
the sensibility of whose mind was of no ordinary character,
arising from the delicacy of her education. The Providence
of God, in causing us to meet with Capt. Furze, led us to
place a stronger confidence in his covenant faithfulness, and
we were prepared to view it as a cup of consolation, on which
was inscribed "Jehovah-jireh," in characters too legible to be
mistaken. It was presented by the hand of paternal and sovereign goodness, and we were led to exclaim, "The Lord reign-
eth, let the earth rejoice." It was determined that, in the
morning, I should accompany Capt. Furze to the house of
Dr. Fleming, at Bedford, one of the gentlemen who wrote
to me in behalf of the congregation. He was a scholar and a
gentleman, and also a farmer who attended to the cultivation
of his farm in person. Bedford had been a frontier town dur-

ing the Revolutionary war, and had suffered from the depre-
dations of both parties. The church, built of wood, and un-
stained by a single brush of paint, and unenclosed, presented
an appearance of desolation exceedingly affecting. Houses
scattered here and there, many of them in a decayed state,
led me to apprehend that the situation could not be very eligi-
ble to me or my family. Suffice it to say, that we arrived at
a decayed dwelling, into which, after having fastened our
horses under an old shed, we entered. We were received with
kindness and hospitality by two young ladies, who were peculiarly neat in their appearance and graceful in their manners. It was Saturday, and the custom of washing their floors
had not been forgotten; and I was not without apprehension
that the wet floor would produce some unpleasant effect upon
my health. Capt. Furze having left the room, I was left alone
in conversation with the ladies, whom I found to be the daugh-
ters of Dr. Fleming. Soon, an individual entered the room,
and, proffering me his hand, "hoped," as he said, "for better
acquaintance." It proved to be Dr. Fleming, who had just
returned from his labor, and was dressed in a manner suited
to his occupation. As I had not been introduced to him, I
considered him to be a common workman. At this you will
not be surprised, when you recollect the rank that English
physicians sustain, and the appearance of the same class of
individuals in the populous towns and villages in this country.
I was, of course, greatly surprised, on the return of Capt.
Furze, to learn that this person was Dr. Fleming. It was
upon him I was principally to depend for introduction to
the people, and I had anticipated finding in him a person of
entirely different appearance. He told me he was very sorry
I had come, and that they already had hired a minister between that congregation and the one at Poundridge. I told
him I was exceedingly surprised at so premature an engagement, for it was in consequence of his invitation that I had
determined to remove from England. He said he wished I
had come earlier. I told him that if he considered the rapidity
with which I had hastened to comply with the invitation, he
would rather wonder that I had come so early, than express
regret that I had come so late. He then asked if I had brought
any testimonials. I replied that, after what had passed, I was

astonished that they considered these necessary, but that I had
them. He then asked if I had called on Dr. Rodgers, in
New York. I told him I had not, having had no letters of
introduction to him, and did not know such a step was necessary. I then inquired the name of their clergyman. He told
me it was Mr. Abner Benedict, a man of sound principles and
of fine character, and that his engagement was for one year.
Capt. Furze now taking his leave for the night, I was left alone
with strangers, to struggle with feelings to which, until this
time, I had been an entire stranger. Their intensity was
indescribable, and, if any expression moved upon my affec-
tions from the prospect which I conceived to be before me, it
was this, "My God, my God, why hast thou forsaken me?"
Supper was now soon prepared and of a material generally
admired as an evening repast in that part of the country. It
was samp. It was a food to which I was not accustomed, and
my head was soon out of the window. The hour being come
for retirement, we committed ourselves to the care of Him
whose eyes never sleep and whose eyelids never slumber. In
my private devotions, I endeavored to seek some token for
good, to enlighten the darkness of the prospect before me and
my family. I traced over what had occurred, and what I had
fondly considered as the indications of an approving Providence, but I could not dissipate the gloom that hung over my
spirits. My eyes were held waking, and my imagination ran
away with my judgment, so that I had not the understanding
of a man, and my faith grew weak from my reflecting upon
the events which had crowded upon me, stranger as I was, in
a strange land. When thinking of my wife and tender babes,
I was overwhelmed with anticipations pregnant with distress,
I presume I suffered a partial delirium, from which I was
aroused by leaping from my bed and striking my head against
the wall. As the day had dawned, I dressed and sought the
open air. Well do I recollect a retreat, some distance from
the house, where no eye saw me but the eye of God, no ear
heard me but His whose presence is everywhere, and who
heareth the young ravens when they cry. Here I endeavored
to pour out my heart to God, and assuage my grief by the
consolations of the gospel. Anxiously did I call to mind, as
the foundation of my hope, such passages as these: "If ye,

then, being evil, know how to give good gifts unto your children, how much more shall your Father which is in Heaven give good things to them that ask him." "Fear thou not; for I am with thee: be not dismayed; for I am thy God." But all was in vain. I was like a mariner at sea in a frail boat, without compass and without chart. The mountain wave rose higher and higher and well-nigh overwhelmed me. I perfectly recollect uttering expressions of discontent toward God and his Providence, so foolish, so sinful was I. I said to the Almighty—if, for want of zeal in the cause of Christ I am brought hither—if, for any thing Thy pure eyes have seen amiss in me, I am brought into circumstances like these, no congregation to bid me welcome, no pulpit from which to declare the unsearchable riches of Christ—what have my beloved family done, who must be sharers in those privations and disappointments in which our voyage has resulted? On returning to the house, I found myself weak and exhausted. It was the Lord's day. In the exercise of family worship I had more of the spirit of prayer, more encouragement to call God my Father, and a greater range of thought than I could have dared to hope for. It afforded a sweet relief to learn hereby, that God did not treat me as a rebellious child, but still permitted me to look upon Him, shedding upon my afflicted heart the expression of His paternal kindness; and, on rising from my knees, methought I heard a voice say, "Stand still, and see the salvation of the Lord." We were soon seated around the table spread with the bounties of Providence. Dr. Fleming and his family were neatly attired, and, howsoever forbidding his manners had been on the previous evening, they this morning presented a perfect contrast. He recommended himself by a politeness of which he was well capable, and a softness of expression which at that time was peculiarly gratifying. In about an hour we were comfortably seated in a wagon on our road to the church, which, was about a mile and a half from the Doctor's residence. When we arrived, we found a large collection of people standing on the outside of the church. To the elders and several others I was introduced. If I had been surprised, at a passing glance, at the exterior of the building, I was much more so on beholding its interior, where was neither plaster, pew, nor gallery. The minister indeed was accommodated with a pulpit, while his hearers sat on slabs, supported by two legs at each end, and two in the middle. Upon one of these I sat down, awaiting the arrival of the clergyman. At length he entered and passed into the pulpit, with an octavo Bible under his arm. His countenance betokened much Christian meekness and benevolence. In this estimate I was not afterwards disappointed. As soon as he was seated in the pulpit, my friend the Doctor ascended the stairs, to inform him, I presume, who the stranger was that sat on the slabs below, as he arose, and, standing on the upper step, kindly invited me to sit with him. For several reasons, however, I declined, but I consented to make the last prayer and preach for him in the afternoon. During the intermission between the services, many of the congregation repaired to a neighboring house, among whom were Mr. Benedict, Dr. Fleming, etc., etc. I was invited to accompany them, and an excellent opportunity was afforded me of laying before them a statement of my circumstances, my invitation, testimonials, etc., etc. Mr. Benedict instantly said, that, in justice and propriety, he must consider his engagement with them at an end, and that he could not in conscience think of retaining a situation that so evidently belonged to his brother just arrived from across the Atlantic. A consultation being held on the subject, it was agreed, that, if the congregation at Poundridge would accede to the measure, both the pulpits should be supplied by an alternation of services by Mr. Benedict and myself. This was a pleasant relief, and I looked at it as an intimation of the good Providence of God being still continued toward me. The exercises of the afternoon were peculiarly acceptable. Esquire McDonald, who was present, kindly offered to accommodate me and my family for the present. I accordingly returned in the morning to Sing Sing landing for them. The awkward situation in which they were placed rendered my presence peculiarly desirable. In compliance with Mr. McDonald's kind invitation, I took my family to his house in Bedford. Several of the members of the congregation at Poundridge had been present at church the preceding Sabbath, and, through them and Mr. Benedict, arrangements were made agreeably to my wishes. These were completed before the close of the week. We soon discovered among the people at

Bedford and Poundridge many affectionate and pious individuals, with whom we could hold familiar and pleasant converse. Some inconveniences as well as trials of feeling had to be encountered, yet the constant assiduity of individuals, and their kind anticipations of our wants, will ever be remembered with sentiments of sincere gratitude toward Him who led their hearts to such acts of beneficence. Although the family of Mr. McDonald were highly hospitable, we considered it of importance, if possible, to obtain a dwelling of our own. But, where should one be found, where all were occupied? The parsonage had been let out on a lease that would not expire till the spring, and, as no better accommodations could be found than two rooms and a kitchen in an old unfinished house, we concluded to remove thither. I bless God that both your dear mother and myself had determined to be content in such a state as God might be pleased to place us in; nor did I ever witness more Christian fortitude than your mother displayed on that occasion. Our servant girl, our faithful Molly,* was almost overcome, and, knowing the comforts which your mother enjoyed before leaving England, could not help exclaiming, "Oh, Mem, how will you ever endure it?" The rooms were unplastered and sided by rough unjointed boards, nailed against the studs, not for the purpose of keeping out the cold, but for the nailing on of the laths when the owner should see fit to do so. We pasted paper over the crevices, and in this manner enclosed ourselves in more comfortable apartments than we had anticipated. We had to borrow some few articles of furniture which could not be purchased, such as a table, two or three chairs, etc., etc. Indeed I had to exercise some of my own ingenuity. I made a table, together with two settees, one of which last we still retain as a memento of that period.

On the 25th of October following our removal, was born Harriet Peacock; † and your dear mother, for whom we had felt so much anxiety, was mercifully supported, and made to

---

* In one corner of the family burial lot, at Oakwood Cemetery, Troy, New York, is a white marble headstone, on which are these words: "Mary Smith, aged 47, our faithful family nurse from 1790 until her death October 3d, 1810."

† Dr. Peacock was the family physician at Totnes, England.

experience the truth of that promise, "As thy days, so shall thy strength be." Surely, my dear children, the mercies of God were new every morning and fresh every evening. Great was His faithfulness.

At the first meeting of the Presbytery of Hudson, within the bounds of which my congregations were, I attended, with the view of laying my testimonials before its members, and enjoying the counsel and countenance of that body. I there met persons whom I shall ever remember with feelings of grateful emotion. The kindness with which they received me, a stranger, can never be forgotten by me. Among them were the Reverend Messrs. King and Close. At this meeting the following was entered on the books of the Presbytery: "The church at Bedford requested the Presbytery to appoint the Reverend Samuel Blatchford a stated supply among them, till the next stated meeting of the Presbytery; upon which, the Presbytery asked Mr. Blatchford whether he was acquainted with and approved of the Confession of Faith, Form of Government, Discipline and Directory for the worship of God, of the Presbyterian Church in the United States, and, upon his answering these questions in the affirmative, the Presbytery did appoint him to supply at Bedford as many Sabbaths as would be convenient."

Early in the succeeding year, 1796, I received an invitation to spend a Sabbath at Greenfield, Fairfield county, Connecticut, where was settled the late Reverend Dr. Dwight, who, by a display of talents of the very first order, diligence, a fine and cultivated taste, and an untarnished character for piety and zeal in his Master's cause, had secured to himself a high reputation. My preaching in this place elicited from the church and congregation an invitation to preach for them, and the following communication was forwarded to me: "At a meeting legally warned and held in the parish of Greenfield, the 1st day of April, 1796—Daniel Sherwood, Moderator. Voted, unanimously, to invite the Reverend Mr. Blatchford, for one year, to preach for said parish. Voted, to give Mr. Blatchford £160 currency, for his services for said year. Voted, to give Mr. Blatchford $20, to defray his expenses in removing to Greenfield. Hezekiah Bradley, Society's Clerk." After taking the advice of my brethren, and spreading the whole affair before the throne of Divine Grace, for direction in the path of duty, I came to the resolution of accepting their invitation, with the privilege of being bound by this agreement no longer than six months, if any circumstance should occur to render my removal desirable. During this period, I was introduced to my excellent friend, Dr. Dwight, who requested me, whenever I came to New Haven, to make his house my home. I was present at the Commencement at Yale College next ensuing, and, at the request of gentlemen belonging to the United Society of Whitehaven and Fairhaven, which pulpits were then vacant, I preached for them a few Sabbaths, by exchange. An intimation was then given that it would be desirable, if it might be done consistently, that I should yield my engagement in Greenfield, and take into consideration the wishes of the people thus informally expressed. This request I thought it my duty not to comply with. I accordingly continued at Greenfield.

Early in the year 1797, I received the following extracts from the records of the proceedings of the Presbyterian Society at Stratfield, Connecticut: "At a meeting of the members of the Presbyterian Society at Stratfield, Conn., legally warned and held at their meeting-house, February 15th, 1797, Joseph Strong, Esq., Moderator, a motion is made, whether the society wish to call a candidate for settlement in the ministry. Voted, they do. Voted, that Richard Hubbell, Deacon Seth Seelye, Stephen Summers, Aaron Hawley, Benjamin Wheeler and Lambert Lockwood, be a committee to look out for a candidate and make report. Voted, this meeting adjourn until Monday next, at 4 o'clock, P. M." "February 20, 1797. Met again, agreeable to adjournment. Moderator being absent, voted, that Capt. Amos Hubbell be Moderator *pro tem.* Motioned, that, from specimens we have had, we admire the Reverend Mr. Blatchford as a preacher, and wish for further opportunity to determine whether it may not appear for mutual good that he take charge of this church and society as pastor. Voted unanimously. Motioned, that our committee for the purpose of looking out a candidate be, and they hereby are, recommended to said Mr. Blatchford, with directions to offer him at the rate of $500 for one year, commencing his labors with us next spring; and, further, we agree, that if after his being with us six months, we do not mutually covenant with him on some more permanent footing, he may either leave us then or continue through the year. Voted unanimously. Meeting adjourned without day. A true copy from the records. Lambert Lockwood, Clerk.''

In the course of a few weeks I received the following, presented by Mr. Jeremiah Atwater: ''New Haven, March 29, 1797. Reverend Sir: The united society of Whitehaven and Fairhaven yesterday had a meeting to consult on the expediency of obtaining a permanent supply of the gospel ministry. On a consideration of the subject, they expressed their approbation of your past, and unanimously united in the desire of your future, labors among them. As they wish, however, not to deviate from duty by interrupting any arrangements you may have made with any other people, they consider it expedient to express their wishes to obtain your ministrations for them six or twelve months, at such future period as your arrangements will admit, and this with a view to eventual settlement, in case, on future acquaintance, duty shall dictate the measure. Uncertain how far it would be proper to make proposals of a more particular kind, until they know whether you have accepted or dismissed the application which you informed our committee you had under consideration, the Society have instructed us, in connection with Mr. Jeremiah Atwater, to express to you their wishes and sentiments, and to make enquiries relative to your engagement. Should our enquiries and the conference with Mr. Atwater enable us to represent to the Society that you are not engaged to any people, and the time it is probable you will be at leisure, the Society will address to you the necessary stipulation for support. Wishing you the Divine direction and extensive usefulness in the work of the ministry, we are, Reverend sir, respectfully, your humble servants, Eleazar Goodrich, Hezekiah Hotchkiss, William Austin.''

The wishes of the people at New Haven were again urged upon me, and, as the time of my engagement at Greenfield was fast drawing to a close, it became necessary for me to decide. Accordingly, after a mature consideration of the subject, I came to the conclusion of accepting the invitation of the congregation at Stratfield, and declining that from New Haven.

My residence at Greenfield was, for the most part, agreeable to your mother's feelings and mine. We enjoyed a society there which was truly delightful. It formed the basis of friendships which have continued to the present time, although death, the great destroyer, hath entered many a family, and torn from the domestic circle friend after friend. Near Greenfield, resided Captain Smedley, who, on hearing of my arrival, hastened thither to express his obligations to my family, and to recognize in me the youth who was the agent, on the part of my uncle and my mother, in affording him relief during his confinement at the house of Mrs. Chenough. Captain Smedley, it will be recollected, was one of those gentlemen who was assisted in his escape to Holland.

At Greenfield, on the 5th of January, 1797, was born Samuel Milford.

I had also succeeded the Reverend Dr. Day, the present President of Yale College, as instructor in an academy at Greenfield, and, previous to my formal acceptance of the invitation from Stratfield, I made some stipulations with the committee from thence, other than those expressed in the call—such as building an edifice proper for an academy, as I was desirous of instructing some youth in classical literature, as an additional means of support for my numerous family. These arrangements being made, I removed to Stratfield. I succeeded in my plans, and the school flourished. I was installed by the Association of Fairfield East, and we all felt happy in our new situation. We occupied a house situated in the western part of the town, commonly called Stratfield or Pequonic.

On the 23d of April, 1798, was born Richard Milford.

In this year we heard of my beloved mother's death. She died in the hope of the gospel, and is doubtless in possession of the inheritance of the saints in light. We soon purchased a house and lot belonging to Stephen Boroughs, in a part of the town called Newfield, afterwards, by act of the legislature, called Bridgeport, belonging to the same Society.

On the 24th of May, 1799, was born John; on the 21st of August, 1800, Sophia; on the 7th of December, 1801, Frederick; and on the 7th of January, 1803, George Edgcumbe.

In January, 1804, I received an invitation to take charge of the Presbyterian churches at Lansingburgh and Waterford, in the State of New York, which invitation I eventually accepted. The field of usefulness here presented was more extended than the one in which I was then laboring, and the means of support offered were more ample, which, on account of my large family, was exceedingly desirable.

I cannot leave this part of my narrative without making mention of my gratitude for the many proofs of cordial friendship with which I was eminently indulged by the ministers and citizens of the State of Connecticut, as far as I was known. The Association with which I was particularly connected, together with the Western Association of Fairfield county, were ever ready to show to me those marks of regard which took from me and my family the idea of being strangers, and greatly compensated for the pain which I felt in being separated from those I held dear in the land of my fathers. Drs. Edwards, Trumbull, Ely and Ripley (the last is still alive), together with Messrs. Eliot, Stebbins, Pinneo, Rexford and Huntington (of Middletown), also Drs. Perkins, Lewis, Burnet, and many others, are among those toward whom the sense of obligation must remain, while kindness can make any impression on my heart. Let the following be considered, among many others, as tokens of that cordial confidence and kindness with which I was regarded by my brethren: At the Commencement at Yale College in the year 1798, I was presented with the honorary degree of A. M. I was also twice appointed by the General Association of Connecticut a delegate to the General Assembly of the Presbyterian Church. I was unable to attend the Assembly when I was first appointed. I considered the repetition of the honor in the year 1801 as a mark of peculiar confidence, since, at that time, it was in the charge of the delegate, if the Assembly should see fit, to consider and digest a plan of government for the churches in the new settlements. The Assembly, according to the plan suggested by the Association, appointed a committee of conference, consisting of the Reverend Drs. Edwards and McKnight, Mr. Hutton, an elder from Albany, and myself. The report, containing the wished-for plan, will be found at large in the Assembly's proceedings for the year 1801. As it proved satisfactory to the Association, it was adopted at the next

RICHARD MILFORD BLATCHFORD

Pencil sketch taken about 1820, after graduation, while tutor in
Chancellor Livingston's family. Copy made by Bierstadt on order of
Edward T. Potter

meeting of the Association and, I believe, has ever been considered a distinguishing blessing to the churches of our Lord Jesus Christ. It has promoted harmony and secured peace, removed impediments in the way of missionary efforts, and exhibited a fine specimen of Christian fellowship. Alas! how often have such lesser differences of church government divided Christians, and torn the seamless robe of Christian charity, which should ever remain untorn and uninjured.

The call presented by the churches at Lansingburgh and Waterford was unanimous. I agreed also to take charge of the Lansingburgh Academy, and the whole of my salary was $1,200. I was installed by the Presbytery of Columbia, on the 19th of July, 1804. The congregation at Waterford had formerly been under the care of the Albany Presbytery; but, through the influence of the Dutch population, a Dutch Reformed church had been built, and, by way of compromise between the Presbyterians and the Dutch, Mr. Close, then of the Presbytery of Hudson, was called to be their pastor. The English population, however, increasing, and difficulties on that account arising, Mr. Close (who was an excellent man, and lived to an advanced age) resigned his pastoral office, and the church, uniting with the Presbyterian church at Lansingburgh, presented me a call.

On the 6th of September, 1804, was born Charles Baynham;* but He who gave and had a right to take away was pleased to remove him from us to His own immediate keeping on the 18th of November in the same year.

On the 23d of November, 1805, was born Ethelinda Jane; and, on the 1st of August, 1807, was born George Edgcumbe 2d.

The foregoing narrative, thus left incomplete, was continued by Thomas W. Blatchford, a son of the Reverend Dr. Blatchford, in the form of a letter addressed to his children, which he prefaced with the following note: "Troy, April 29th, 1848. To T. Wickes Blatchford, Samuel T. Blatchford, John T. Blatchford, and Harriet W. Blatchford. My dear children: Believing that it will be interesting to you, if not now, certainly at some future day, to know something more of your grandfather than is contained in the foregoing most interesting narrative, I have concluded to add a few particulars in the form of a

---

* Charles Baynham, Esq., was a friend of the Reverend Dr. Blatchford's, in Devonshire, England. He subsequently came to this country and resided in Bridgeport, Connecticut.

letter addressed to you. If the remembrance of those in whom piety and learning and enterprise unite is worth cherishing, the virtues and excellences of your dear grandfather should not soon be forgotten. Your affectionate father, Thomas W. Blatchford.''

Thus far your sainted grandparent had proceeded in his autobiography, when death terminated his earthly engagements by summoning him to scenes of unmingled joy and heavenly activity. Your aunt Jane, now Mrs. P. M. Corbin, who acted as his amanuensis upon this occasion (for the above sketch was dictated from the bed of death), states that the closing sentence recording the birth of his sixteenth child, George Edgcumbe, 2d, was the last sentence he ever dictated upon any subject. She says that she waited for him to finish the sentence, but he seemed lost in thought. After a short time, he said he would stop for the present, and go on again bye and bye. Although he confidently calculated to resume and complete what, after much entreaty from all his children, he had thus begun, his Heavenly Father had determined otherwise, for, in less than thirty hours from this period, his tongue was silent in death. This circumstance renders the closing words the more remarkable. It seems as if the dear Saviour, whom he had so long and faithfully served, condescended to favor him with a little foretaste—a slight glimpse, as it were —of those joys He knew he was so soon to realize, and thus enable him, in sweet anticipation, to dwell upon the happy meeting about to take place with his own dear ones who had preceded him to glory.

You will perceive that he brought his history down to the period of his removal from Bridgeport and his entrance upon the laborious duties connected with his settlement in Lansingburgh. Twenty-four years of his useful life are thus left unnoticed, from his thirty-eighth to his sixty-second year.

The fact that some of the inhabitants of Lansingburgh were natives of Bridgeport and Fairfield, and were already well acquainted with his character, probably conduced to his removal to Lansingburgh. The father of Mr. Seth Seelye, the present senior elder of the church in Lansingburgh, was one of the deacons of the church at Bridgeport. Mr. Eli Judson was from Fairfield, and his brother, David Judson, Esq., was one of your grandfather's warmest friends. But the gentleman most instrumental in bringing it about was David Allen,

THE OLD LANSINGBURGH CHURCH
Of which Rev. Samuel Blatchford was pastor from 1804 to 1828

Esq., also from Fairfield, whose kindness and attention were always unremitting, and in whose death, in 1825, your grandfather sustained a severe loss.

The Academy at Lansingburgh, among the oldest endowed by the Regents, had, for some time, been in a declining state, and had now dwindled to almost nothing, chiefly from the want of a competent head—a Principal whose talents and acquirements could impart confidence to the public. The two churches of Lansingburgh and Troy had, since their organization in 1793, been united under the ministry of the Reverend Jonas Coe, afterwards Dr. Coe. The congregation in Troy, increasing in numbers and strength, proposed a separation, and, it being concurred in by the congregation at Lansingburgh, invited Mr. Coe, in 1803, to give them his undivided services, which he did until his lamented death, in 1822. In a letter I received from your grandfather, dated August 2d, 1822, he says: "I presume you have heard of the death of Dr. Coe. His departure is felt as a great loss by the congregation and his numerous friends. I preached his funeral sermon by request. It is supposed upwards of three thousand persons crowded into the church and that there were nearly as many without. Twenty-five ministers were present to pay his memory respect." He was a most estimable man, distinguished for his faithful, unwearied performance of pastoral visitation. This gave him great influence among his people. Between Dr. Coe and your grandfather there was always the closest bond of union and friendship. They were truly brethren. Mr. Coe's withdrawal from his charge at Lansingburgh left the church destitute of a pastor. The trustees of the Academy and the officers of the church and congregation determined mutually to improve this period and seek for a gentleman whose literary and theological attainments would enable him acceptably to discharge the duties of Principal of the Academy and pastor of the congregation.*

---

* The church edifice of Lansingburgh was rebuilt on a different site, in 1844. A marble tablet was inserted at the left side of the pulpit, in the new building, with the following inscription: "In memory of Samuel Blatchford, D. D., for 24 years pastor of this church—Born at Plymouth Dock, England, August 1, 1767—Died in this village, March 17, 1828. The memory of the just is blessed."

A Presbyterian church had been organized in Waterford, but, from feebleness, was not sustained, and had long become, as it were, amalgamated with a Dutch church previously organized under the direction of the Classis of Albany. The Reverend John Close, of the Presbytery of Hudson, was the pastor. The increasing infirmities of age compelled him to resign his charge in part, at least, when the Presbyterian church was again organized, occupying the Dutch edifice, and receiving pecuniary aid from the Dutch members. It united with the church and Academy at Lansingburgh, in extending a call to your grandfather, who already enjoyed high reputation as a preacher of the gospel and an instructor of youth. Thus, in reality, three bodies united in the enterprise—the officers of the Academy and the two congregations. The following are the names of the gentlemen authorized to extend the invitation: William Bell, Matthew Harrison, Thomas Bassle, elders; James Hickok, David Allen, Elijah Janes, trustees. Not one of them is now living.

Your grandfather's first visit to Lansingburgh was performed in the winter of 1803-4, on horseback, in company with Mr. Samuel Penny, then a merchant of Bridgeport, and his nearest neighbor. The privations they endured on the road were very trying, and long afterwards formed the subject of many an interesting story in the family circle. They were four days in reaching Lansingburgh.

George Edgecumbe, 2d, whose name occurs in the closing sentence of the memoir, as having been born August 1st, 1807, and whose death your dear grandfather seemed to be contemplating, when he so abruptly ceased to dictate, leaving the sentence half finished, died August 24th, 1808, being a little over a year old. But the family was called to pass through a much severer trial just previous to this event, in the severe and protracted sickness of Alicia and her death. She died on the 21st of April, 1808, of a peculiar disease of the throat, which prevented her from taking food for the last six weeks of her life, her wasting frame being sustained by nourishing enemata. Her sufferings were, for the most part, excruciating.

When I notice the birth of his Benjamin—as he loved to call his youngest son—Edgecumbe Heath, on the 24th of

March, 1811, the record of his seventeen children is complete. Eight of them went before him, ready to welcome him to the abodes of the blessed. Two of them died in England, five in Lansingburgh, and one in Maryland. Harriet Peacock died in her 24th year, and the Reverend Henry Blatchford in his 34th year. The others died in early infancy, except Alicia, whose death I have already noticed.

Having long observed the difficulties which beginners in Greek experienced from the want of a good Greek grammar, with an English instead of a Latin translation, he, soon after his settlement in Lansingburgh, and after consulting with several friends, especially the Reverend Dr. Nott, of Union College, undertook the task of rendering into English the Latin of Dr. Moor's Greek grammar, deeming that, after examining several others, the best of which he had any knowledge. Besides translating it, he furnished notes to it, and added Dr. Ewing's Syntax, in an appendix. A large edition, 2,000, I think, was printed, on his account, in New York, by Collins & Perkins, in 1807. This translation, in the time of it, was held in considerable estimation, and several of our colleges adopted it as their class-book, especially Union College. After a while, however, it was superseded by others, but it is believed to have been the first attempt to teach the Greek grammar in the English language. The fact that the grammar he selected, though improved and honored by another translation, (that of the Reverend Peter Bullions,) is still among the most approved grammars now in use, and the further fact, that, in this country, at least, Latin translations are nowhere put into the hands of beginners, are an honorable tribute to the correctness of your grandfather's judgment.*

---

* In addition to this Grammar, nine sermons and addresses of Rev. Samuel Blatchford were published, as follows: 1. Sermon on "The Nature and Necessity of the New Creation," in 1792. 2. Sermon on "The Great Duty of Universal Love," in 1793. 3. Sermon, "The Validity of Presbyterian Ordination Maintained," in 1798. 4. "Address to the Indians," in 1810. 5. Sermon preached before the Albany Bible Society, on "The Excellency of the Scriptures," in 1811. 6. Address to Soldiers, in 1812. 7. Thanksgiving Sermon, in 1815. 8. Sermon preached in Hudson, N. Y., at the ordination of Rev. Benjamin F. Stanton, in 1817. 9. Sermon, "The Sanctification of the Sabbath," in 1825.

In 1805 he was chosen one of the trustees of Union College, in the prosperity of which institution he always took a very deep interest. Soon after his election, he commenced acting as one of the Board of Examiners, in company with the late Drs. Coe and Proudfit. The duties of this position he continued to discharge until a short time before his death, and he was seldom, if ever, absent from his post. He took pleasure in these semi-annual visitations, and, while he was faithful to his trust, he was uniformly kind and courteous to the students under examination. These examinations afforded him the opportunity of becoming acquainted with many gentlemen who, in after life, distinguished themselves in their various professions, and of forming acquaintances which were mutually pleasant and profitable.

In 1824, he took a deep interest in the organization and prosperity of the Rensselaer Polytechnic Institute, of which he was the first President. The acknowledgment of Mr. Van Rensselaer's indebtedness to him, "not only for the constant encouragement afforded, but for wise counsel concerning the detail and execution of the plan itself," was handsomely expressed in a letter received from Mr. Van Rensselaer, from Washington, when he heard of his severe illness, in 1828. The letter enclosed a munificent donation, "not as a remuneration for services rendered, but as a small token of lasting indebtedness." I was present when the letter was received, and witnessed the effect it had upon your grandfather's feelings. It could not but be grateful to him, coming from such a source, and accompanied by a proof of friendship so substantial. I regret that the letter cannot now be found, or I would copy the original entire, instead of drawing upon my memory for an extract.

In 1808, Williams College, of which the late Dr. Fitch was then President, conferred upon him the degree of Doctor of Divinity. He felt highly honored by this unsought and unexpected mark of respect from those who were comparatively strangers to him.

When speaking of his settlement in Lansingburgh, I ought to have mentioned that, for four years, he continued unremittingly to discharge the duties of Principal of the Academy and pastor of the united congregations of Lansingburgh and

Waterford—united only in ministry, not in government, the elderships being distinct. Such constant employment, notwithstanding the assistance of two faithful ushers, proved entirely too arduous, and, besides, left him but little time for pastoral visitation and attendance upon the sick. In 1809, at his earnest request, an arrangement was entered into, by which he was to spend one-half of the usual amount of time in the Academy. This arrangement continued for two years. By a subsequent arrangement, he engaged to spend one day in the week in the business of instruction, and selected Wednesday as the day most convenient for him, his weekly lecture evening in Waterford being Tuesday, and in Lansingburgh Thursday. In 1811, he withdrew entirely from the institution, except as a trustee. He was elected a trustee some time before his withdrawal as an instructor, and continued to act as President of the Board until just before his death, ever maintaining a lively interest in an institution which, mainly through his instrumentality, had again assumed an honorable standing among kindred institutions.

When first settled over the united churches, he spent the entire Sabbath alternately in each village, preaching twice. After the relinquishment of half of his time in the Academy, he divided the day between the two places, giving the morning to one village and the afternoon and evening to the other, and *vice versa* the next Sabbath. His practice was to write one sermon a week, which he usually delivered in both places, and to preach from short notes or extemporaneously at other times, when he did not avail himself of previous preparation. Saturday was his study day. He must not then be interrupted, except for some very important consideration. He usually went into his study soon after breakfast, and spent the entire day in looking over authors, etc., not commencing his sermon until he had mastered his subject. When he began to write he continued without any cessation until he reached the "improvement." This he frequently left unfinished, except the "heads" of remarks. It is rare that any one of the many sermons he has left exhibits any marks of alteration, any interlining, or any change of expression. It came at once finished from his hands, and fit for the press, as far as it went. The most of Saturday night he thus spent in writing, frequently not retiring to bed until one or two o'clock. His rule was to finish his preparation when he began.

His habits were very studious. He took but little exercise. Most of his time was spent in study. History, especially ancient history, was his delight. His reading was never of a light character. He abhorred the whole class of novels, and for much of that which is called light literature he seemed to have no taste. He could read fluently the Greek, Hebrew and Latin languages, and understood, so as to translate, the Sanscrit and the Arabic. Of the Italian, the French and the Spanish he had but a slight knowledge. He could translate them, but not without difficulty. He wrote a beautiful hand and always prided himself on his penmanship. He could write sixteen different hands.

His taste for the fine arts was above mediocrity. He was very fond of drawing, and has left behind him several specimens of his skill in this department, which are very well executed. This was his favorite recreation.

He was always punctual in his attendance upon the judicatories of the church. Being a strict disciplinarian, he regarded it as an imperative duty to attend all the meetings of Presbytery and Synod, allowing nothing but providential interposition to interfere. He was very seldom absent, no matter how considerable the mere inconvenience or how great the distance. By his Presbytery he was very frequently appointed as Commissioner to the General Assembly. He was chosen Moderator of that body in 1813; and the next year, according to usage, he preached before it. His text was Daniel, 12th chapter, 3d verse. In 1817, the last Moderator not being present, he was selected to preach the opening sermon, and took his text from Ephesians, 1st chapter, 21st and 22d verses. His familiarity with church government and his thorough acquaintance with the proceedings of ecclesiastical courts, together with his acknowledged judgment in all ecclesiastical matters, made him a sort of umpire father in church difficulties, great weight being always attached to his opinions.

His general health was remarkably good. He had some peculiarities of constitution, some idiosyncrasies, from which he occasionally suffered inconvenience. He could not endure,

MRS. ALICIA WINDEATT BLATCHFORD

without sickness or fainting, the sight or smell of a cat, or the taste or smell of cheese; and the smell of vinegar was very offensive to him.

His health began to fail about two years before his death. He had a large tumor in the right side of his abdomen. Most of the physicians whom he consulted pronounced it an enlarged liver. A *post mortem* examination proved it to be an enormous expansion of the kidney, weighing, when removed, fourteen pounds, and six pounds, after evacuating the fluid it contained, which was a sort of bloody serum. The size of this tumor, interfering with the healthy performance of the various functions connected with the organs of digestion, rendered his sickness very protracted. He was confined to his room for about six months, and mostly to his easy chair or his bed. He suffered greatly from the swelling of his legs and body. This rendered him very helpless, and the sympathetic irritation of his stomach was so great that he could retain next to nothing on it. I copy the following from the last letter he wrote to me, and the last, I believe, he ever dictated, with the exception of the one he wrote to Mr. Peters, respecting the Home Missionary Society, and which was published in the organ of that Society immediately after his death: "Lansingburgh, January 4th, 1828. My dear Thomas: I have constituted your dear sister Jane my amanuensis, with a view of communicating a few matters relative to myself. I still continue, as you may perceive, in the land of the living, if this land may, indeed, deserve the appellation, where sickness, sin, and death crowd the shores, and the earth is filled with corruptible bodies. I still wait the command of Him in whose hand are the destinies of man, and feel that I have abundant cause to bless God that I am not exercised with acute pain, and have long intervals of ease. Surely the means you were led to adopt were under the direction of Him who does not willingly afflict nor grieve the children of men. The course which you prescribed I am still pursuing, and the nourishment which I take agrees excellently well with my stomach, and my inclination to it is as good as when you left us. My legs, indeed, continue to swell, but I am free from those distressing spasms to which I was liable, and I am become a stranger to those copious bilious discharges which you witnessed when here. In affording me such relief, the Lord enables me to attend to such services as have for their object the welfare of precious, immortal souls and the glory of God. Sometimes, I am enabled, with great enlargement of spirit, to speak of the wonders and mysteries of grace to small classes of people, and, I trust, in some instances, not without effect upon them, and with sensible refreshing to my own soul. It is delightful, as I approach eternity, to have an evidence or two, brightened up by the light of God's countenance, and the sweet influences of His spirit, before I shall be brought to see Him face to face, and with whom I shall be everlastingly satisfied, when I awake in his likeness.'' He then gives an interesting account of the baptism of Dr. Tucker's son, performed by him on his sick bed, giving his own name. This was the last time he administered this ordinance, and the whole scene was described as one of surpassing solemnity.

Frequently during his protracted confinement, and when his sufferings were not too great, he was in the habit of addressing circles of from five to fifteen or twenty young persons, upon the great object of their eternal concerns, accompanied by singing and closing with prayer. It is known that these solemn and interesting seasons were blessed to the conversion of several of the young persons thus addressed.

He had no ear for music, and could scarcely distinguish one tune from another, yet he greatly enjoyed the singing of others, especially in the social circle.

Just before his death, your aunts determined, without his knowledge, to note down on paper observations which fell from him, from time to time, in his intercourse with those who came to see him. We always regretted that this was not earlier thought of, for, at times, he would give utterance to sentiments of the most touching and sublime character. A few only have been preserved, and I shall finish this letter by transcribing these detached sentences.

To a brother in the ministry he remarked: ''In the garden of the Lord, his laborers are variously occupied. Some busy themselves in planting trees, some in watering and cultivating the delicate and beautiful flowers, and some in pulling up weeds; and thus various is their employment in erecting his glorious temple. The late John Flavel preached regularly,

THE LANSINGBURGH HOME

once a year, to a congregation forty miles from his place of
residence. At an intermediate place, a minister asked to be
dismissed from his people, because his labors had not been
blessed to the conversion of sinners. Mr. Flavel visited this
congregation during one of his journeys, and, on the subsequent evening, requested them to state publicly the benefit they
had derived from their minister's instructions. One said,
he had been relieved in temptation; another had had his hopes
brightened; a third was confirmed in the faith; and all expressed some good done. The minister was overcome with
joy at this expression of satisfaction on the part of his people,
and said, with emotion, 'It is enough, it is enough.' Mr.
Flavel then inquired of his friend, which he thought the most
honorable employment—that of digging the rough stones out
of the quarry, or trimming and preparing them for the building.''

To a company of young converts who had just been received
into the church, and who, by request, visited him a few days
before his death, he observed: ''Let us all walk in a straight
way, like the beams of the sun. They turn neither to the
right hand nor to the left. The people of God have prayed for
a revival, and, when they saw you stand before the altar, a
thrill of joy went to their hearts. A large company have
already gone to Heaven. Remember, you are a band following after. Soon you shall meet together around the throne.
Some of you may have no earthly parent; but, if you have a
Father in Heaven, all will be well. 'When my father and my
mother forsake me, then the Lord will take me up.' You see
how much I suffer. Bodily health is truly a great blessing,
but it is as dear Dr. Watts said, when dying—'All is now
well with me;' and immediately he fell asleep in Jesus.''

To a valued member of his congregation he said: ''We
have long been looking for you to come out from the world.
In former times, men could not make a profession of religion,
without the risk of having their goods pillaged, and their
bodies burned; but you, my dear sir, are not called upon to be
a martyr. It is the tree of life that is before you, and all you
have to do is to reach forth your hand and partake freely of
the fruit, for there are none to molest or make you afraid.''

Soon after this interview, the gentleman alluded to united with the church; and he has long been a ruling elder.

"I have always been a moderate man, or, at least, I have tried to be so; but, in some things, I have been vastly too moderate. God has said, 'Thou shalt love the Lord thy God with *all* thy heart,' but, oh! how often have I suffered a little bit of the creature to creep in, even in my best moments."

"Heaven grows brighter and brighter, as I approach its portals." Then, smiling, he continued: "At times, it dazzles my sight, by the brightness of its glory."

One of his elders observed to him, that his body was decaying fast. "Yes," said he, smiling, "let it decay, let it waste, no matter how fast." Then, with an elevated voice, he exclaimed: "I am ready. Oh! the righteousness of Jesus Christ; 'tis the only way to the living temple."

To another of his elders he said: "Oh! I am truly a great sufferer; but, if I can evince to my people that there is a consolation in religion, which the world can neither give nor take away, I am willing to suffer anything. I am but one of the little children in my Father's family; but He attends as quickly to the cry of the babe, as to the expressed wish of the older ones, and is just as ready to fly to their relief, as a father pitiful and kind."

When in great pain he said: "Oh! that I could speak of my mercies with as much energy as I speak of my distresses." Again: "Oh! what shall I do? The Lord knows; and should not that be enough for me? I do not know that it becomes me much to inquire at all. That is nature, that is nature." Then, with great firmness: "'All the days of my appointed time will I wait till my change come.' Hush, my impatient spirit."

At another time, when in great distress: "But it is all mercy; and what would I have more? I am like a spoiled child. If I am not dandled on the knee, I am continually crying out. What must I do? Not contented with the common fare of the family, I must be cherished in the arms or patted on the cheek."

When supposed to be near his end, he said: "I shall soon forget everything relating to time, except that I was a great sinner, and was made a monument of grace."

To Mrs. Bela Redfield, who expressed herself distressed by the troubles of the church in Troy, he observed: "I have set aside all the contentions and distractions of the church, and look away to the general assembly and church of the first-born in Heaven. *You* have got a new pastor," (referring to Dr. Tucker)—"be careful and do not set your heart too much on the creature. You need not so much regard the streams, while you have free access to the fountain itself."

When feeling very languid, and thinking he was near his end, he said: "Don't let me slip away without telling me of it, for I want to see the little stream I have so soon to cross."

On waking, and appearing much agitated, we observed to him that he had only been dreaming. "Yes," said he,

'This world's a dream, an empty show
But the bright world to which I go
Hath joys substantial and sincere;
When shall I wake and find me there?
Oh for some bright and peaceful bower,
Where sin hath neither place nor power.'

There, there will be none of these sufferings; but the sweetest thought is, that, in Heaven, not a shadow of imperfection or frailty will pass over my sanctified spirit. Oh! Eternity, eternity! Continually advancing from pure to purity itself —from enjoyment to ecstacy."

The approaching Sabbath being Communion Sabbath, he asked: "Where am I to pass my Communion Sabbath?" Some one said: "Perhaps in glory." "Yes, I hope so, and, more, I expect it. Let us see, to-morrow is the preparation day, is it not?" He was told—no—it was Tuesday. "Ah, well! that is right. God does all things well."

Speaking of the kind attentions of his friends, he remarked: "'What!' said our blessed Saviour, when in his agony— 'what! Could ye not watch with me one hour?' Now, I have more mercies than my Divine Master had, since *my* friends give me no opportunity to complain; for they watch by me all the while, every hour."

"Peter had never known the omnipresence of God, had he not begun to sink; so we never know the love, mercy, goodness, and power of God, until we are brought into some serious difficulty.''

"Oh! what a fullness there is in the Lord Jesus Christ! Enough, enough, for all, and still more. I was forcibly struck by a remark which I once heard the Reverend Mr. Reynolds, of London, make, in a sermon: 'When I go through Leadenhall Market,' said he, 'and see the quantity and variety of the provisions which are there exposed, I wonder how it can all be consumed; and then, when I walk through this vast city and contemplate the numbers of its inhabitants, I wonder where the provision is to come from to supply so many wants.' And, now, for the application. Notwithstanding the immense number of His children and the extent and demands of His family, there is provision enough in the Lord Jesus Christ for all; yea, and for ten thousand times ten thousand more, if He should see fit to create them. The poor prodigal was right when he said: 'How many hired servants of my father's have bread enough and to spare.' Oh! for a spiritual appetite.'' Then, addressing himself to one of his sons, he continued: "He will, by His own hand, lead me to His table. Yes, He has; and more than once too. Oh! my son, what a book the Bible is! what a book the Bible is!''

When the day was breaking, and the light began to make its way through the crevices of the closed windows, he observed: "How like the dark mist of early day are all our views here, even the best of them; but, when the sun is up, it will quickly dispel them all, and we shall see things clearly. My sun is rising now, and soon all mist will be vanished; but I must not be impatient.''

While looking at his feet, which were very much swollen, and which seemed about to mortify, he said: "The Lord doth all things well. It is all just as it should be; but, to nature, the waters of Jordan have an unpleasant chilliness.''

"Under what obligations I am to sing the royalties of grace. I say 'royalties' because they all come from the hand of a sovereign.''

A female friend sent to him a request that he would pray for her. After assenting, he continued: "My poor prayers! my poor prayers! I hope she is a Christian and has an intercessor before the throne. Tell her to go to Him.''

To the Reverend Mr. Butler, Rector of St. Paul's church, Troy, he said: "You know that delightful passage, 'The foundation of God standeth sure, having this seal—the Lord knoweth them that are His.'" "Then, your faith is strong," said Mr. B. He replied, with great emphasis: "Yes; yes." "You believe you are His?" "Yes, oh! yes. I would not relinquish my evidence for all this world." "You trust in the merits of your Redeemer?" "Yes, I trust alone in the righteousness of the Lord Jesus Christ."

"I have noticed, when passing up and down the North river, in the steamboat, that there is always a great interest manifested among the passengers to get a good view of the house on Catskill Mountain, and each one wants the loan of the telescope; and, if there were twenty glasses on board, they would all be in requisition to examine more distinctly the distant edifice. So, we, who are sailing down the river of life, have, as it were, a mountain house to contemplate—a building of God—that house not made with hands, eternal in the heavens; and we, too, blessed be God, have a telescope of divine origin—the word of God, through which we may examine the beautiful building, and view its foundations, and admire its structure and its extent, and from which we have the privilege of learning the qualifications necessary for admittance there. Oh! the Bible! the Bible! what a treasure is the Bible!"

To his youngest son, who, in an hour, expected to make a public profession of religion, being seventeen years of age, he observed: "This is a solemn day to you, my son; and, although I am debarred the precious privilege of leading you to the altar myself, yet I bless God you will have a standing there. Look through, I beseech you, look through the elements to the body and blood of the Lord Jesus Christ. Ever remember that it is not a mere profession that constitutes the hope of a Christian, but the blood of Christ. Then, give yourself all away." After making a short and affecting prayer, he threw his arms around his neck and kissed him.

"If any of the ransomed of the Lord will be permitted to sing, 'Not unto us, O Lord, not unto us, but unto Thy name give glory,' I shall be among that number."

To a very aged member of his congregation, a merchant,

who had never yet seen his way clear to make a profession of religion, he remarked: "If you come in at the eleventh hour, my word for it you shall not lose your penny. Life is short; death is sure; it behooves you to be diligent. The light is almost out; the wick is already in the socket; it will soon flicker for the last time. It is a pearl of great price that is hid in the gospel field, and that merchant is divinely wise who makes that pearl his own."

"My flesh, you see," speaking to some of his children, "is failing fast, and I am fast going down to the grave; but, blessed be God, I can look beyond without one distressing fear. I find myself on a rock, when trusting to the righteousness and blood of Christ; and I think I can set my feet in Jordan, and not be afraid. It is but a narrow stream and may soon be crossed. Oh, what a sweet privilege to stand on gospel ground, and look within the veil. If I did not do this, the very stones would cry out. Yes, it is sweet; and the higher we stand on gospel ground, the richer are the beauties we behold. I can mount a little, like the eagle; and, like the lark, I can chirp, though feebly. I have seen the lark rise from the green meadow, singing as he rose, and mounting upward until he appeared a mere mote in the sunbeam. I could not but think he taught me that it was my own fault if I did not know more of the sublimities of religion. Oh! for heavenward aspirations!"

"This is sometimes a privileged chamber. I must believe that the Lord is here. Oh! the goodness of God! I see His mercy in everything—yes, even in the pain I suffer."

"Oh! what a glorious plan is the plan of salvation! Here I am now, confined to this poor decaying body; and soon I hope to be as active and free as any seraph around the throne. Look at the penalty: 'In the day that thou eatest thereof, thou shalt surely die.' But the curse is made a blessing."

One morning, being very low, he appeared, for some minutes, lost in deep thought, and then, suddenly, broke out with much energy of expression, and said:

> " 'Jesus, my God, I know His name,
> His name is all my trust,
> Nor will He put my soul to shame,
> Nor let my hope be lost.'

No, I have a heavenly confidence in His faithfulness, His ability, His love. Oh! my children, be not too solicitious for this poor, suffering, dying body. I have a glorious view—a glorious anticipation—of what is in store for me. I now see Him by faith. Soon, oh! soon, I shall see Him face to face." After a few moments' silence, he added: "Oh! I have had a Pisgah's view."

Addressing a young man who had been thoughtful for some time, but who seemed to be halting as to duty, and whom he had before urged to immediate repentance, he said: "L——, my dear friend, religion is something or it is nothing. If it is nothing, then let it float on the imagination, like a bubble on the stream; but if it is something, remember, it holds in its grasp the keys of Heaven or of Hell. Embrace it, and you are a child of glory. Reject it, and you are a fiend of Hell."

"O, thou, that dwelleth in the heavens, where Peter and Paul, David and Manasseh, and all the redeemed, ascribe honor and power and glory to the Lamb, shall I be permitted to bow among them there? O Lord, I am thine, do Thou take me to thyself."

To Mr. Seelye, one of his elders, he said: "I have been wonderfully supported hitherto, and I trust I shall be until I get home to my Father's house. We may weep at our temporary separation, but we shall have abundant cause to rejoice when we meet again. I am not ashamed of the gospel I have preached. It is the plain gospel of Jesus Christ." He then again repeated the lines, "Jesus, my God, I know His name," etc. "I bless God now, that I have been kept from those vagaries in theology, which can never be reconciled nor explained, in which the glory of God is hid. It is picking at the shell and neglecting the kernel."

"'As thy days, so shall thy strength be.' I am weak, very weak, but the Lord, by his assistance, supports the very staff he gives me; else, it would drop from my hand."

One morning, when considered near his end, he thus addressed one of his kind physicians: "Doctor, I am waiting my Father's will, I am watching for the messenger; and now, my dear sir, I embrace this opportunity of telling you, my hope is fixed on the righteousness and blood of the Lord Jesus Christ. That gospel I have so long preached I now find all

sufficient for my support. Permit me, sir, again to recommend
the religion of the Lord Jesus Christ to your immediate acceptance. Put your trust in Christ. He was the God of your
departed father, He is the God of your sainted mother, and
His everlasting arms are stretched out ready to receive you
also; and they are embossed with the blood of the Redeemer.
Reject and perish; accept and you are a child of glory.''

To two brethren in the ministry, who enquired of him his
feelings in view of death, he said: ''I feel a rapture in my
own mind, and am led to exclaim, The Lord God of my salvation liveth. I feel like a passenger waiting patiently for the
hour of departure to arrive. I always felt unpleasantly at
the idea of leaving my family and going from home; but,
somehow or other, I look upon the journey of eternity, if I
may so express myself, with a holy delight. I feel like going
home. Everything here is polluted; hence, it cannot be the
Christian's rest. Faith and hope, as sister graces, accompany
me all the way, and direct my eye to the infinite rest above;
and soon, they will beckon to me and say, Come up hither.
The hope of glory which Christ has formed within me, is by
the glorious administration of the spirit of grace.''

Upon being told of the revivals with which God was so
extensively blessing His church, he said: ''I bless God that I
have been spared to see such a glorious day in the church.
The praise cannot be of man, or of one set of men. It
must be all of God, for the work is not confined to one part
more than another of the field; but, in every portion we behold the glorious triumphs of the Redeemer.''

To some young ministerial brethren, who said they felt it
a privilege to visit him in his sick chamber, after telling them
something of his joys and anticipations, and most affection-
ately urging them to be faithful to their trust, and reminding
them of the solemnity of their ordination vows, he said:
''Go forth with the standard of the Cross. Hold it up, what-
ever may oppose. Some will turn away from its attractive
beauty; but still go on—discharge your duties in the strength
of the God of Jacob, and He will bless you.''

Towards the close of his life, he became subject to severe
paroxysms of pain and spasm. After one of these, which
seemed peculiarly severe, he said, with an inexpressible smile

upon his countenance: "As the wise men of the East were traveling in pursuit of the babe Jesus of Nazareth, they were guided in their course by the star of Bethlehem, which grew brighter and brighter as they went, until it stood over the place where the child lay. If I am permitted to have the sight of that star, even in its glimmering state, how happy am I. It is this star that strengthens, supports, and encourages me as I go to be with Christ. But, oh! how shall such a poor sinner as I am bear the sight of the overwhelming glory of my Divine Redeemer? I cannot, surely, unless sanctified more and more by the spirit of His grace." Then, with great emphasis, he added: "But this shall be so, and it will be to the praise of His rich and sovereign grace."

Feeling very languid, and perceiving his feet covered with a cold sweat, he said: "As I feel the chilling drops of the spray of Jordan gathering on my feet, how could I meet him who is falsely called the king of terrors, as my friend, were it not for the rich support afforded me by the sovereign grace of Him who conquered death, hell, and the grave, when He rose triumphant from their grasp."

When urged to take a little nourishment, having taken nothing for some time, he remarked, cheerfully: "My eating days are almost over, but my banquet days are all before me. Oh! Eternity, Eternity!

> 'When shall I pass the dreary night
> In the bright realms of heavenly light.' "

During a paroxysm of pain, and when he groaned out, "Oh! what shall I do? what shall I do?" he suddenly stopped, and then, composing himself, said:

> " 'Does it behoove me much to know
> What I'm to suffer here below,
> While God directs my longing eyes
> To the bright world beyond the skies.' "

To his family he remarked: "If I am not in the hands of the arch-deceiver, my hope in the covenant grows stronger and the star of Bethlehem increases in brightness. Aye, and it will continue to do so, until it becomes the sun of righteousness to my enraptured soul."

When taking a little drink, and while holding the tumbler, he said: "Oh! how many cups of mercy have I, without any thing offensive floating on the top. Shall I complain, then, if, occasionally, a little bitter is mixed with it? No, Lord, no. Thy will be done."

"Prayer is a bank note drawn upon the great proprietor— sure pay, no failure."

"We love to receive letters from absent friends. The word of God is his book of letters to his absent children."

After an interesting interview he had enjoyed with Dr. Nott, he said to his family, when they returned to his room: "Oh! was there ever so full a cup of mercy poured out at the feet of a poor dying sinner as has now been administered to me.

'Lord, I am thine, but thou wilt prove,' " etc.

After recovering from one of his severe paroxysms, he said: "It is harder crossing the stream than I had anticipated; but the beauties of Canaan are not in the least diminished by the tediousness of the passage."

At another time, after a similar paroxysm, he looked up, and, smiling, said, very deliberately: " 'He hath done all things well,' was a label inscribed upon His crown when on earth, and all the malignity of earth and hell combined has never yet been able to pluck it hence."

The above is enough to show you how a Christian and a Christian minister can die. For two or three weeks after he was first seriously ill and when he began to realize the fatal nature of the disease under which he was laboring, he suffered a good deal of mental darkness and depression. He was greatly troubled respecting the doctrine of the resurrection, but it pleased his Heavenly Father to clear up all his doubts upon every subject, and after this, for months, he had no ground for dejection. His hope was always bright, his faith always strong, but he loved to dwell on a "risen Jesus," as he used to express himself; and few individuals were ever permitted to enjoy richer foretastes of the rest remaining to the people of God. For twelve hours before his death he was in a lethargic state, and scarcely recognized any thing; but his work was all done and well done. His evidences of a happy change had already been so indelibly recorded upon the memory of friends, that no expression he could have made, had he been favored with his senses, would have added any thing to their assurances that his hopes of Heaven were well founded.

It is the desire of my heart that you, my dear children, may follow him as far as he followed Christ, and that, when our earthly course is finished, we may meet him in his own happy home in Heaven.

That this may be the case, is the sincere and constant prayer of

Your affectionate father,
THOS. W. BLATCHFORD.

your Affectionate Mother
Alicia Blatchford

FIRST GENERATION

1. HENRY BLACHFORD died in the parish of St. Judy, Cornwall, England (will dated May 17, 1747; proved July 24, 1747); married, probably, Grace Symonds whose burial is recorded in St. Judy's Register, September 26, 1780, thus, "Grace Blatchford, aged 75;" resided in Devonshire, England.

SECOND GENERATION

2. HENRY BLATCHFORD,[2] son of Henry Blachford, died October 10, 1781, in his 63rd year, at Plymouth Dock, Devonshire, England; married first, Honor ——————— who was buried February 28, 1755, at St. Judy, Cornwall, England; married second, July 17, 1766, in the Parish Church of Stoke Damrell, Devonshire, England, Mary Heath of Totnes, born in 1735, died 1798, daughter of Robert Heath* and Mary Alford. She married second, October 23, 1783, at Stoke Damrell, James Howell, shipwright.

CHILDREN:

By first marriage:
3.   I.   John Blatchford.
By second marriage:
4.   II. Samuel Blatchford, born Aug. 1, 1767; married Alicia Windeatt.+
5.   III. Jane Blatchford, married Christopher Burns of Plymouth Dock.
6.   IV. Joseph Blatchford, died aged five years.
7.   V.   William Blatchford, died in infancy.

---

* See Appendix A.

61

THIRD GENERATION

3. REV. SAMUEL BLATCHFORD,[3] D. D. (Henry,[2] Henry [1]), son of Henry Blatchford and Mary Heath, was born August 1, 1767, at Plymouth Dock [since called Devenport] Devonshire, England; died March 17, 1828, at Lansingburgh, New York; married March 25, 1788, in England, Alicia Windeatt, born November 19, 1767, at Bridgetown, Totnes, Devonshire, England; died December 2, 1846, at Lansingburgh, N. Y., daughter of Thomas Windeatt ‡ of Totnes, Devonshire. By profession, clergyman, Presbyterian, D. D. Williams.*

CHILDREN:

8. I. Henry Blatchford, born Dec. 4, 1788; married Mary Ann Coit.+

9. II. Mary Milford Windeatt Blatchford, born Jan. 24, 1790, at Frogmore, Devonshire, England; died Aug. 17, 1847, at Lansingburgh, N. Y.

    * "Mary Milford Windeatt, daughter of Sam'l and Alice Blatchford, born 24 Jan. 1790, was baptized 17 May, 1790, by Robt. Winton."

10. III. Alicia Windeatt Blatchford, born Feb. 14, 1791, at Topsham, Devonshire, England; died April 21, 1808, at Lansingburgh, N. Y.

    * "Alice Windeatt Blatchford, daughter of Sam'l and Alice Blatchford, born 14 February, 1791, was baptized 17 May, 1791, by Robt. Winton."

11. IV. Sarah Blatchford, born April 23, 1792, at Topsham, Devonshire, England; died June 23, 1793, at Topsham.

    * Sarah Blatchford, daughter of Sam'l and Alice Blatchford, was baptized June 28, 1792 (born 23 April, 1792), by Robt. Winton."

‡ See Appendix B.

* A Memorial Window is in the Lansingburgh Presbyterian church, in memory of Samuel Blatchford, D. D., Pastor, 1804-1828.

12.   V.   Samuel Blatchford, born May 3, 1793, at Topsham, Devonshire, England; died Feb. 3, 1794, at Topsham.

> * "Samuel Blatchford, son of Samuel and Alice Blatchford, was baptised June 23, 1793, by Robt. Winton."

13.   VI.   Thomas Windeatt Blatchford, born July 20, 1794; married Harriet Wickes.+

14.   VII.   Harriet Peacock Blatchford, born Oct. 25, 1795, at Bedford, N. Y.; died March 18, 1819, at Lansingburgh, N. Y.

15.   VIII.   Samuel Milford Blatchford, born Jan. 5, 1797; married Betsey Hunt Kellogg.+

16.   IX.   Richard Milford Blatchford, born April 23, 1798; married first, Julia Ann Mumford; married second, Angelica Hamilton; married third, Katharine Hone.+

17.   X.   John Blatchford, born May 24, 1799; married Frances Wickes.+

18.   XI.   Sophia Blatchford, born Aug. 21, 1800, at Newfield, Conn.; died Feb. 14, 1875, at Troy, N. Y.

19.   XII.   Frederick Blatchford, born Dec. 7, 1801; married first, Almira Jones; married second, Harriet (Hatch) Myers.+

20.   XIII.   George Edgecumbe Blatchford, born Jan. 7, 1803, at Bridgeport, Conn.; died May 3, 1805, at Lansingburgh, N. Y.

21.   XIV.   Charles Baynham Blatchford, born Sept. 6, 1804, at Lansingburgh, N. Y.; died Nov. 18, 1804, at Lansingburgh, N. Y.

22.   XV.   Ethelinda Jane Blatchford, born Nov. 23, 1805; married Pliny M. Corbin.+

---

* NOTE:—"Copied verbatim from the register of the Presbyterian Chapel at Topsham, Devonshire, England, in the handwriting of Reverend Samuel Blatchford, to each of which his name is signed."

23. XVI. George Edgecumbe Blatchford, born Aug. 1,
            1807, at Lansingburgh, N. Y.; died Aug. 24,
            1808, at Lansingburgh, N. Y.
24. XVII. Edgecumbe Heath Blatchford, born March 24,
            1811; married Mary Ann Hubbard.+

Henry Blatchford

Nassau Hall July 1st 1814.

FOURTH GENERATION

8. Rev. Henry Blatchford [4] (Samuel,[3] Henry,[2] Henry [1]), son of Rev. Samuel Blatchford and Alicia Windeatt, was born December 4, 1788, at Ford, Devonshire, England; died September 7, 1822, at Princess Anne, Maryland; married September 10, 1817, Mary Ann Coit, born January 21, 1798, at New York City; died July 20, 1869, at Liverpool, England; daughter of Elisha Coit, Esq. of New York City, and Rebecca Manwaring. She married, second, Samuel Hubbard.* By profession, clergyman, Presbyterian, M. A. Union College, Schenectady.

Children:

25.   I.   Rebecca Coit Blatchford, born July 26, 1818; married Marshall Sears Scudder.+

26.   II.   Harriet Alicia Blatchford, born Feb. 26, 1820, at Salem, Mass.; died March 6, 1820, at Salem.

27. III.   Alicia Harriet Blatchford, born June 1, 1821; married Charles William Scudder.+

13. Thomas Windeatt Blatchford [4] (Samuel,[3] Henry,[2] Henry [1]), son of Rev. Samuel Blatchford and Alicia Windeatt, was born July 20, 1794, at Topsham, Devonshire, England; died January 7, 1866, at Troy, New York; married February 3, 1819, Harriet Wickes, born May 25, 1789, at Huntington, Long Island, New York; died April 12, 1875, at Troy, New York; daughter of Thomas Wickes, Esq., of Jamaica, Long Island, New York. M. D., College of Physicians and Surgeons, New York.

Children:

28.   I.   Thomas Wickes Blatchford, born Feb. 20, 1820; married Jane Bunce Smith.+

---

* See Appendix C.

67

29.   II.   Samuel Blatchford, born March 4, 1822; married
            Agnes Euphemia Leadbeater.+
30. III.   John Thomas Blatchford, born June 18, 1823, at
            Jamaica, Long Island, N. Y.; died, date and
            place unknown.
31.   IV.   George Edgecumbe Blatchford, born Jan. 26, 1825,
            at Jamaica, Long Island, N. Y.; died Oct. 5,
            1828, at Troy, N. Y.
32.   V.   Harriet Wickes Blatchford, born May 8, 1828 at
            Jamaica, Long Island, N. Y.; died Aug. 18, 1828,
            at Troy, N. Y.
33.   VI.   Harriet Wickes Blatchford, born Feb. 21, 1829, at
            Troy, N. Y.; died Aug. 28, 1896, at Troy, N. Y.

15. SAMUEL MILFORD BLATCHFORD [4] (Samuel,[3] Henry,[2]
Henry [1]), son of Rev. Samuel Blatchford and Alicia Windeatt,
was born January 5, 1797, at Greenfield, Connecticut; died
June 3, 1864, at New York City; married April 19, 1819, Bet-
sey Hunt Kellogg; born June 11, 1799, at New Canaan, Con-
necticut; died February 24, 1873, at Bay Ridge, Long Island,
New York; daughter of Samuel Kellogg, Esq. of New York.
Occupation, merchant.

CHILDREN:

34.   I.   Alicia Harriet Blatchford, born Jan. 31, 1820;
            married Nathaniel Fuller Hopkins.+
35.   II.   Henry Samuel Blatchford, born June 3, 1823;
            married Martha Crossman.+
36. III.   James Wilson Blatchford, born May 8, 1825; mar-
            ried first, Emeline W. Smith; married second,
            Rosina Jenkins.+
37.   IV.   Samuel Milford Blatchford, born Oct. 25, 1835;
            married first, Abby Catharine Townsend; mar-
            ried second, Henrietta (Tilden) Swan.+

16. RICHARD MILFORD BLATCHFORD [4] (Samuel,[3] Henry,[2]
Henry[1]), son of Rev. Samuel Blatchford and Alicia Windeatt,
was born April 23, 1798, at Stratfield, Connecticut; died September 3, 1875, at Newport, Rhode Island; married first, May
17, 1819, Julia Ann Mumford, born July 24, 1798, at New

Thos W Blatchford

Troy 28 August 1846

York City, died December 23, 1857, at New York City, daughter of John P. Mumford, Esq., of New York; married second, November 8, 1860, Angelica Hamilton, born November 13, 1819, at New York City, died November 10, 1868, at New York City, daughter of James A. Hamilton, Esq., of Nevis, Westchester County, New York; married third, January 18, 1870, Katharine Hone, born January 9, 1819, at New York City, died June 12, 1901, at New York City, daughter of Philip Hone, Esq., of New York. Profession, Counsellor at Law; Member of the New York Assembly, 1885; Counsel for the Bank of England; appointed by Lincoln, 1862, U. S. Minister at Rome; LL. D., Union College, Schenectady.

CHILDREN:

38. 1. Samuel Blatchford, born March 9, 1820; married Caroline Frances Appleton.+

39. II. Mary Milford Blatchford, born Oct. 29, 1823; married Burr Wakeman Griswold.+

40. III. Julia Alicia Blatchford, born Aug. 9, 1830, at New York City; died Nov. 25, 1831, at New York City.

41. IV. Julia Maria Blatchford, born Oct. 4, 1834; married Edward Tuckerman Potter.+

42. V. Sophia Ethelinda Blatchford, born May 25, 1836, at New York City; died Oct. 1, 1908, at Newport, R. I.

17. JOHN BLATCHFORD [4] (Samuel,[3] Henry,[2] Henry [1]), son of Rev. Samuel Blatchford and Alicia Windeatt, was born May 24, 1799, at Newfield, Connecticut; died April 8, 1855, at St. Louis, Missouri;* married May 18, 1825, Frances Wickes, born May 12, 1805, at Jamaica, Long Island, New York, died January 8, 1875, at Chicago, Illinois, daughter of Eliphalet Wickes, Esq., of Jamaica. By profession, clergyman, Presbyterian; college president; D. D., Marion College.

---

* A double Memorial window is in the First Congregational church of Bridgeport, Conn., in memory of Samuel Blatchford, D. D., Pastor, 1797-1804, and John Blatchford, Pastor, 1830-1836.

CHILDREN:

43. I. Eliphalet Wickes Blatchford, born May 31, 1826; married Mary Emily Williams.+

44. II. Richard Milford Blatchford, born Aug. 20, 1827, at Stillwater, N. Y.; died Feb. 20, 1832, at Bridgeport, Conn.

45. III. Martha Wickes Blatchford, born June 17, 1829; married Morris Collins.+

46. IV. John Samuel Blatchford, born Jan. 19, 1831, at Bridgeport, Conn.

47. V. Frances Alicia Blatchford, born Sept. 6, 1832, at Bridgeport, Conn.; died June 6, 1846, at Oakland Green, near West Ely, Mo.

48. VI. Eliza Allen Blatchford, born Sept. 22, 1834, at Bridgeport, Conn.; died June 11, 1835, at Bridgeport.

49. VII. Harriet Punnett Blatchford, born May 9, 1837, at Jacksonville, Ill.; died Aug. 7, 1838, at Chicago, Ill.

50. VIII. Eliza Harriet Blatchford, born Nov. 21, 1838, at Chicago, Ill.; died March 3, 1839, at Chicago.

51. IX. Alexander Blatchford, born Jan. 1, 1840, at Wheeling, Va.; died Oct. 9, 1847, at Hazeldean, near Quincy, Ill.

52. X. Mary Cebra Blatchford, born Oct. 23, 1843, at Marion College, Mo.; died Dec. 27, 1849, at Hazeldean, near Quincy, Ill.

53. XI. Alice Windeatt Blatchford, born Dec. 20, 1847, at Hazeldéan, near Quincy, Ill.; died Aug. 6, 1892, at Chicago, Ill.

54. XII. Nathaniel Hopkins Blatchford, born Sept. 25, 1849; married first, Ella Marion Philbrick; married second, Helen De Reimer Wheeler.+

19. FREDERICK BLATCHFORD [4] (Samuel,[3] Henry,[2] Henry [1]), son of Rev. Samuel Blatchford and Alicia Windeatt, was born December 7, 1801, at Bridgeport, Conn.; died October 6, 1883, at Oberlin, Ohio; married first, January 6, 1823, at Utica, New York, Almira Jones, born September 5, 1803, at Great

SAMUEL MILFORD BLATCHFORD

Barrington, Massachusetts, died May 23, 1865, at West Ely, Missouri, daughter of Solomon Jones of Litchfield, Connecticut; married second, November 23, 1866, at Chicago, Ill., Harriet (Hatch) Myers, widow of Rev. Joseph Myers, of Syracuse, New York, born April 12, 1801, at Coventry, Connecticut, died April 6, 1877, at Syracuse, New York, daughter of Daniel Hatch. Occupation, farmer.

CHILDREN:

55. I. George Edgecumbe Blatchford, born Nov. 5, 1825; married Lydia Melvina Overton.+

56. II. Sarah Jane Blatchford, born July 6, 1837, at Brooklyn, N. Y.; died Aug. 14, 1838, at Troy, N. Y.

57. III. Mary Jane Blatchford, born Aug. 23, 1838; married William Berger Watson.+

58. IV. Frederick Anson Blatchford, born Oct. 6, 1839, at Brooklyn, N. Y.; died Sept. 16, 1840, at Lansingburgh, N. Y.

59. V. Almira Blatchford, born May 27, 1842; married Thomas Wilbur.+

60. VI. Sarah Julia Blatchford, born June 14, 1845; married William Henry Harrison Morriss.+

22. ETHELINDA JANE BLATCHFORD [4] (Samuel,[3] Henry,[2] Henry[1]), daughter of Rev. Samuel Blatchford and Alicia Windeatt, was born November 23, 1805, at Lansingburgh, New York; died September 13, 1879; married May 18, 1847, Pliny Moore Corbin, born December 8, 1801, at Craftsbury, Vermont, died November 29, 1874, at Troy, New York, son of Royal Corbin, Esq., of Craftsbury, Vermont. Occupation, banker.

CHILD:

61. I. Alicia Blatchford Corbin, born Sept. 27, 1848; married Edward Judson.+

24. EDGECUMBE HEATH BLATCHFORD [4] (Samuel,[3] Henry,[2] Henry[1]), son of Rev. Samuel Blatchford and Alicia Windeatt, was born March 24, 1811, at Lansingburgh, New York;

died February 14, 1853, at New York City; married October 26, 1837, Mary Ann Hubbard, born September 7, 1820, at Brookline, Massachusetts, died July 25, 1864, at Cambridge, Massachusetts, daughter of Hon. Samuel Hubbard of Boston, Massachusetts. By profession, lawyer; M. A., Union College, Schenectady.

CHILDREN:

62.   I. Mary Edgecumbe Blatchford, born Aug. 13, 1838, at New York City.

63.   II. Ethelinda Jane Blatchford, born Jan. 12, 1841; married Samuel Hubbard Scudder.+

64. III. Alicia Windeatt Blatchford, born Jan. 8, 1843, at New York City; died April 28, 1845, at New York City.

65.   IV. Grace Vernon Blatchford, born May 13, 1845, at New York City; died Oct. 24, 1861, at Cambridge, Mass.

66.   V. Caroline Hubbard Blatchford, born June 10, 1851, at New York City; died March 27, 1896, at Waverly, Mass.

R.M.Blatchford
N. York. Sely 30. 1859.

25. REBECCA COIT BLATCHFORD [5] (Henry,[4] Samuel,[3] Henry,[2] Henry [1]), daughter of Rev. Henry Blatchford and Mary Ann Coit, was born July 26, 1818, at New York City; married July 24, 1839, Marshall Sears Scudder, born May 31, 1818, at Boston, Massachusetts, died August 26, 1875, at Boston, Massachusetts, son of Charles Scudder, Esq., of Boston. No children.

27. ALICIA HARRIET BLATCHFORD [5] (Henry,[4] Samuel,[3] Henry,[2] Henry [1]), daughter of Rev. Henry Blatchford and Mary Ann Coit, was born June 1, 1821, at Lansingburgh, New York; died September 14, 1892, at Marblehead Neck, Massachusetts; married August 16, 1841, Charles William Scudder, born January 4, 1820, at Boston, Massachusetts, died December 20, 1891, at Brookline, Massachusetts, son of Charles Scudder, Esq., of Boston.

CHILDREN:

67.   I.   Francis Henry Scudder, born March 30, 1842; married Sarah Rollins Trufant.+

68.   II.   Henry Blatchford Scudder, born June 18, 1844; married Julia Randolph Perry.+

69.   III.   Winthrop Saltonstall Scudder, born July 26, 1847; married first, Caroline Augusta Townsend; married second, Jeanette Sumner Willoughby.+

70.   IV.   Mary Windeatt Scudder, born May 24, 1851, at Brookline, Massachusetts; died September 14, 1853, at Westboro, Massachusetts.

71.   V.   Bessie Marshall Scudder, born Oct. 1, 1853, at Brookline, Massachusetts; died May 2, 1899, at Worcester, Mass.

28. THOMAS WICKES BLATCHFORD [5] (Thomas W.,[4] Samuel,[3] Henry,[2] Henry [1]), son of Thomas Windeatt Blatchford and Harriet Wickes, was born February 20, 1820, at Jamaica, Long Island, New York; died August 23, 1863, at Troy, New York; married November 9, 1847, at Brooklyn, New York, Jane Bunce Smith, born April 12, 1830, at Brooklyn, New York; died October 15, 1865, at Smithtown, Long Island, New York, daughter of Jeffrey Smith, Esq., of Brooklyn.

CHILD:

72.　I.　Amy Blatchford, born Sept. 4, 1855; married Samuel Dwight Wilcox.+

29. SAMUEL BLATCHFORD [5] (Thomas W.,[4] Samuel,[3] Henry,[2] Henry[1]), son of Thomas Windeatt Blatchford and Harriet Wickes, was born March 4, 1822, at Jamaica, Long Island, New York; married December 27, 1848, Agnes Euphemia Leadbeater, born October 2, 1824, at Mount Pleasant, New Jersey, daughter of Edward Leadbeater, Esq., of New York.

CHILDREN:

73.　I.　Thomas Windeatt Blatchford, born Sept. 3, 1851, at New York; died Jan. 7, 1856, at Troy, New York.

74.　II.　Kate Blatchford, born Oct. 3, 1853, at Federal Store, New York; died July 29, 1857, at Brooklyn, N. Y.

75.　III.　Thomas Windeatt Blatchford, born Jan. 24, 1857; married Susie Carter.+

76.　IV.　Richard Milford Blatchford, born Aug. 7, 1859; married Natalie Cary Green.+

34. ALICIA HARRIET BLATCHFORD [5] (Samuel M.,[4] Samuel,[3] Henry,[2] Henry [1]), daughter of Samuel Milford Blatchford and Betsey Hunt Kellogg, was born January 31, 1820, at Utica, New York; died June 6, 1893, at Bay Ridge, Long Island, New York; married December 1, 1841, Nathaniel Fuller Hopkins, born July 2, 1809, at Hanover, New Hampshire, died August 19, 1851, at Staten Island, New York, son of Daniel Hopkins, Esq., of Salem, Massachusetts. Occupation, merchant.

Dr. Blatchford
1823

CHILDREN:

77. I. Samuel Milford Blatchford Hopkins, born Sept.
          19, 1842, at New York City.

78. II. Susan Ten Brook Hopkins, born Jan. 14, 1844, at
          New York City.

79. III. Henry Coman Hopkins, born May 2, 1845; married
          Susan Wells Kent.+

80. IV. Mary Emerson Hopkins, born Feb. 24, 1847, at
          New York City.

81. V. Sarah Lothrop Hopkins, born Dec. 28, 1849, at
          New York; died Sept. 8, 1850, at Staten Island,
          New York.

82. VI. Nathaniel Fuller Hopkins, born Sept. 10, 1851;
          married first, Caroline Adams; married second,
          Clara Appel.+

35. HENRY SAMUEL BLATCHFORD [5] (Samuel M.,[4] Samuel,[3]
Henry,[2] Henry[1]), son of Samuel Milford Blatchford and
Betsey Hunt Kellogg, was born June 3, 1823, at Utica, New
York; died February 3, 1869, at New York City; married
June 17, 1844, Martha Crossman, born January 25, 1826, at
Cincinnati, Ohio, died January 6, 1892, at Branch Hill, Ohio,
daughter of William Crossman, Esq., of Cincinnati.

CHILDREN:

83. I. Richard Milford Blatchford, born June 12, 1845;
         married Amelie Kancher.+

84. II. Helen Alicia Therése Blatchford, born November
         27, 1849; married Charles Rule.+

36. JAMES WILSON BLATCHFORD [5] (Samuel M.,[4] Samuel,[3]
Henry,[2] Henry[1]), son of Samuel Milford Blatchford and
Betsey Hunt Kellogg, was born May 8, 1825, at New York
City; died at New York City; married first, June 12, 1850,
Emeline Smith, born May 26, 1832, at New York City, died
July 22, 1855, at New York City, daughter of G. Washington
Smith, Esq.; married second, April 6, 1858, Rosina Jenkins,
born January 27, 1826, at Lancaster, Pennsylvania, died Janu-
ary 21, 1904, at Queens, Long Island, New York, daughter of
William Jenkins, Esq., of Lancaster.

CHILDREN:

85. I. Sarah Lothrop Blatchford, born May 20, 1852, at New York City; died July 24, 1852, at Long Branch, New Jersey.
86. II. William Kirkland Lothrop Blatchford, born Oct. 20, 1853, at New York City; died Feb. 8, 1857, at Staten Island, N. Y.
87. III. Pattye Lane Blatchford, born Jan. 27, 1859, at New York City.
88. IV. Ellen Julia Blatchford, born Dec. 28, 1866, at New York City.

37. SAMUEL MILFORD BLATCHFORD [5] (Samuel M.,[4] Samuel,[3] Henry,[2] Henry[1]), son of Samuel Milford Blatchford and Betsey Hunt Kellogg, was born October 25, 1835, at New York City; died December 3, 1897, at New York City; married first, November 20, 1883, at Newport, Rhode Island, Abby Catharine Townsend, born October 15, 1847, at Newport, Rhode Island, died December 29, 1890, at New York City, daughter of Edmund J. Townsend, Esq., of Newport, Rhode Island; married second, September 5, 1893, at Pittsfield, Massachusetts, Henrietta (Tilden) Swan, born September 21, 1845, at New Lebanon, New York, daughter of Henry Augustus Tilden, Esq., of New Lebanon, New York. No children.

38. SAMUEL BLATCHFORD [5] (Richard M.,[4] Samuel,[3] Henry,[2] Henry[1]), son of Richard Milford Blatchford and Julia Ann Mumford, was born March 9, 1820, at New York City; died July 7, 1893, at Newport, Rhode Island; married December 17, 1844, Caroline Frances Appleton, born August 27, 1817, at London, England, died June 12, 1901, at New York City, daughter of Eben Appleton, Esq., of Lowell, Massachusetts. By profession, lawyer; private secretary to Gov. William H. Seward, 1840; United States District Judge, New York, 1867; United States Circuit Judge, New York, 1878; United States Supreme Court Justice, Washington, 1882.

CHILD:

89. I. Samuel Appleton Blatchford, born Sept. 9, 1845; married Wilhelmina Bogart Conger.+

and grandchildren

Harriet Almira   *Kate Dallas.*

August 4th 1847

39. MARY MILFORD BLATCHFORD [5] (Richard M.,[4] Samuel,[3] Henry,[2] Henry [1]), daughter of Richard Milford Blatchford and Julia Ann Mumford, was born October 29, 1823, at New York City; died February 14, 1852, at Milwaukee, Wisconsin; married June 18, 1851, Burr Wakeman Griswold, born September 5, 1823, at Goshen, Connecticut, died June 1, 1886, at New York City, son of Rev. Darius Oliver Griswold, of Saratoga, New York. No children.

41. JULIA MARIA BLATCHFORD [5] (Richard M.,[4] Samuel,[3] Henry,[2] Henry [1]), daughter of Richard Milford Blatchford and Julia Ann Mumford, was born October 4, 1834, at New York City; married March 3, 1856, at New York City, Edward Tuckerman Potter, born September 25, 1831, at Schenectady, New York, died December 21, 1904, at New York City, son of Right Reverend Alonzo Potter, D. D., Bishop of Pennsylvania, and Sarah Maria Nott. By profession, architect.

CHILDREN:

90. I. Julian Potter, born Aug. 10, 1858; married Alice Pixley.+

91. II. Ethelinda Potter, born Nov. 20, 1860; married Howard Nott Potter.+

92. III. Edward Clarkson Potter, born Aug. 11, 1862; married Emily Blanche Havemeyer.+

93. IV. Robert Francis Potter, born May 17, 1864, at New York City.

94. V. Richard Milford Blatchford Potter, born Dec. 1, 1869, at Paris, France; died Nov. 8, 1901, at New York City.

95. VI. Louisa Millicent Windeatt Potter, born Feb. 7, 1872; married first, Joseph Earl Sheffield; married second, William Adams Delano.+

96. VII. Julia Selden Potter, born July 29, 1875; married Tompkins McIlvaine.+

43. ELIPHALET WICKES BLATCHFORD [5] (John,[4] Samuel,[3] Henry,[2] Henry [1]), son of John Blatchford and Frances Wickes, was born May 31, 1826, at Stillwater, New York; married October 7, 1858, at Chicago, Illinois, Mary Emily Williams, born June 16, 1834, at Hadley, Illinois, daughter of John Chandler Williams, Esq., of Chicago, and Mary Martin Moore. Occupation, manufacturer.

CHILDREN:

97.   I.   Paul Blatchford, born July 18, 1859; married Frances Veazie Lord.+

98.   II.   Amy Blatchford, born May 20, 1862; married Rev. Howard Sweetser Bliss.+

99.   III.   Frances May Blatchford, born May 25, 1865, at Ulmenheim, Chicago, Ill.

100.   IV.   Edward Williams Blatchford, born July 13, 1868, at Ulmenheim, Chicago.

101.   V.   Florence Blatchford, born Jan. 24, 1872, at Evanston, Ill.; died June 4, 1874, at Evanston.

102.   VI.   Charles Hammond Blatchford, born Jan. 2, 1874; married Carita Tyler Clark.+

103.   VII.   Eliphalet Huntington Blatchford, born Oct. 9, 1876, at Ulmenheim, Chicago; died December 23, 1905, at Winnetka, Illinois.

45. MARTHA WICKES BLATCHFORD [5] (John,[4] Samuel,[3] Henry,[2] Henry [1]), daughter of John Blatchford and Frances Wickes, was born June 17, 1829, at Stillwater, New York; died May 19, 1862, at Hartford, Connecticut; married November 4, 1852, at Hazeldean, near Quincy, Illinois, Morris Collins, of St. Louis, Missouri, born October 18, 1813, at Blandford, Massachusetts, died March 19, 1873, at Jacksonville, Illinois, son of Amos Morris Collins, Esq., of Hartford, Connecticut. Morris Collins married second, May, 1865, at St. Louis, Missouri, Hannah Aurelia Adams, born June 2, 1838, at Fitzwilliam, New Hampshire, died March 26, 1898, at Kansas City, Missouri, daughter of John Sabin Adams, Esq., of Fitzwilliam. Their child, Henry Adams Collins, born February 6, 1866, at St. Louis, died August 19, 1867, at Jacksonville, Illinois.

CHILDREN:

104.   I.   John Blatchford Collins, born Sept. 7, 1853; married first, Nellie Davis; married second, Nellie Rebecca Thompson.+

Williamstown July 30 1873
Your Mother
E. I. Corton

105. II. Frances Wickes Collins, born Dec. 25, 1854, at St. Louis, Mo.; died Jan. 3, 1859, at St. Louis.

106. III. Mary Lyman Collins, born Sept. 1, 1856, at St. Louis, Mo.; died Dec. 22, 1858, at St. Louis.

107. IV. Amos Morris Collins, born Nov. 25, 1857; married Charlotte Brown Young.+

108. V. Martha Blatchford Collins, born July 12, 1859; married John Franklin Downing.+

109. VI. Alice Blatchford Collins, born Nov. 30, 1860, at Hartford, Conn.

110 VII. Richard Ely Collins, born May 9, 1862, at Hartford, Conn.; died Sept. 5, 1862, at Wethersfield, Conn.

54. NATHANIEL HOPKINS BLATCHFORD [5] (John,[4] Samuel,[3] Henry,[2] Henry [1]), son of John Blatchford and Frances Wickes, was born September 25, 1849, at Hazeldean, near Quincy, Illinois; married first, May 18, 1872, at Concord, New Hampshire, Ella Marion Philbrick, born May 16, 1849, at Pittsfield, New Hampshire, died April 29, 1899, at New York City, daughter of Richard N. Philbrick, of Concord; married second, August 12, 1901, at Ripon, Wisconsin, Helen de Reimer Wheeler, born December 28, 1859, at Berlin, Wisconsin, daughter of Ezra Wheeler, Esq., of Mount Upton, New York. Occupation, manufacturer.

CHILDREN:

111. I. Agnes Blatchford, born Sept. 21, 1873, at Evanston, Ill.; died April 23, 1884, at Chicago, Ill.

112. II. Francis Wickes Blatchford, born Sept. 20, 1875; married Frances Greene Larned.+

113. III. Luther Morrell Blatchford, born Jan. 31, 1878. at Chicago; died June 24, 1888, at Chicago.

114. IV. Nathaniel Hopkins Blatchford, born Nov. 21, 1883, at Chicago.

55. GEORGE EDGECUMBE BLATCHFORD [5] (Frederick,[4] Samuel,[3] Henry,[2] Henry [1]), son of Frederick Blatchford and Almira Jones, was born November 5, 1825, at Oran, New York; died April 25, 1898, at Monarch, Chaffee County, Colorado;

married December 4, 1856, at Yellow Springs, Ohio, Lydia Melvina Overton, born December 4, 1826, at Westfield, New York, died November 10, 1905, at Albuquerque, New Mexico, daughter of Luther Overton, Esq., of Mineral Point, Wisconsin. No children.

57. MARY JANE BLATCHFORD [5] (Frederick,[4] Samuel,[3] Henry,[2] Henry [1]), daughter of Frederick Blatchford and Almira Jones, was born August 23, 1838, at Brooklyn, New York; died April 21, 1909, at Honolulu, Hawaiian Islands; married September 6, 1865, at West Ely, Missouri, William Berger Watson, born August 23, 1836, at New York City, son of John Watson of West Ely, Missouri.

CHILDREN:

115. I. Harriet Almira Watson, born Sept. 2, 1867, near West Ely, Mo.; died unmarried, Feb. 16, 1898, at Maunaola Seminary, Makawao, Mauii, Hawaiian Islands.

116. II. Kate Dallas Watson, born Feb. 14, 1872; married William Joseph Forbes.+

59. ALMIRA BLATCHFORD [5] (Frederick,[4] Samuel,[3] Henry,[2] Henry [1]), daughter of Frederick Blatchford and Almira Jones, was born May 27, 1842, at Little Union, Missouri; died November 24, 1900, at Denver, Colorado; married May 18, 1865, near West Ely, Missouri, Thomas Wilbur, born September 17, 1839, at Fall River, Massachusetts, son of Thomas Wilbur, M. D., of Fall River.

CHILDREN:

117. I. Kate Sarah Wilbur, born July 23, 1866, at Ralls, Mo.; died Sept. 4, 1867, at Ralls, Mo.

118. II. Annie Morris Wilbur, born May 21, 1869; married Wilbur Truman Liggett, M. D.+

119. III. Frederick Blatchford Wilbur, born Sept. 25, 1871, at Hannibal, Mo.

120. IV. Louisa Briggs Wilbur, born Sept. 18, 1874; married Garrett Benton Hudnutt.+

E. H. Blatchford –
Dec 2. 1835 –

60. SARAH JULIA BLATCHFORD [5] (Frederick,[4] Samuel,[3] Henry,[2] Henry [1]), daughter of Frederick Blatchford and Almira Jones, was born June 14, 1845, at Little Union, Missouri; died September 25, 1890, at Pueblo, Colorado; married May 4, 1865, at "Milford," near West Ely, Missouri, William Henry Harrison Morriss, born August 24, 1840, at Philadelphia, Missouri, son of Henry Morriss of Lewis County, Missouri.

CHILDREN:

121.   I.   Allie Morriss, born Oct. 17, 1868; married James Edgar Day.+

122.   II.   Edwin Wilbur Morriss, born Feb. 8, 1871; married Lydia Frances Courtney.+

123.   III.   Rosalie Morriss, born July 23, 1874; married Reuben Delos Sprague.+

124.   IV.   Anna Belle Morriss, born Aug. 20, 1876; married Harold Arthur Sprague.+

125.   V.   Frederick Blatchford Morriss, born Apr. 28, 1878; married Ida Marie Bower.+

126.   VI.   William Milford Morriss, born Feb. 28, 1880; married Ada Lee Murray.+

127.   VII.   Clara Grace Morriss, born Aug. 16, 1882; married Dec. 20, 1908, at "Hawthorne Home," near Bethel, Mo., Forest Milton Darr, born April 22, 1873, at Emerson, Mo., son of Samuel Joseph Darr, of Emerson. Their daughter, Lillian Darr, was born Nov. 11, 1910, at Emerson.

128.   VIII.   Elsie Winifred Morriss, born July 2, 1890, at Pueblo, Colo.; married Jan. 23, 1910, James Levi Brown, born Oct. 3, 1886, at Benbow, Mo., son of James Stephen Brown of Benbow; resides at Philadelphia, Mo.

61. ALICIA BLATCHFORD CORBIN [5] (Ethelinda J.,[4] Samuel,[3] Henry,[2] Henry [1]), daughter of Ethelinda Jane Blatchford and Pliny Moore Corbin, was born September 27, 1848, at Lansingburgh, New York; married April 26, 1876, at Troy, New York, Edward Judson, born January 20, 1840, at Seneca Falls, New

York, son of Rev. Aaron Judson (Presbyterian clergyman, died at Oswego, New York, August, 1852) and Sophronia Mason.

CHILDREN:

129. I. Ethelinda Blatchford Judson, born Feb. 16, 1877, in Troy, N. Y.

130. II. Helen Judson, born Feb. 5, 1879, in Lansingburgh, N. Y.

131. III. Ruth Judson, born Feb. 5, 1879, in Lansingburgh, N. Y.; died August 25, 1879, in Lansingburgh.

132. IV. Alexander Corbin Judson, born Dec. 21, 1883, in Lansingburgh, N. Y.

133. V. Marjorie Mason Judson, born June 21, 1885, in Castile, N. Y.

63. ETHELINDA JANE BLATCHFORD [5] (Edgecumbe H.,[4] Samuel,[3] Henry,[2] Henry [1]), daughter of Edgecumbe Heath Blatchford and Mary Ann Hubbard, was born January 12, 1841, at New York City; died June 9, 1872, at Montreux, Switzerland; married June 25, 1867, Samuel Hubbard Scudder, born April 13, 1837, at Boston, Massachusetts, died May 17, 1911, at Cambridge, Mass., son of Charles Scudder, Esq., of Boston.

CHILD:

134. I. Gardiner Hubbard Scudder, born Sept. 3, 1869, at Cambridge, Mass.; died Dec. 26, 1896, at Cambridge.

Sam'l Blatchford

Washington, Oct' 27th 1892

SIXTH GENERATION

67. FRANCIS HENRY SCUDDER [6] (Alicia H.,[5] Henry,[4] Samuel,[3] Henry,[2] Henry [1]), son of Alicia Harriet Blatchford and Charles William Scudder, was born March 30, 1842, at Boston, Massachusetts; married June 11, 1867, at Bath, Maine, Sarah Rollins Trufant, born September 7, 1843, at Bath, Maine, daughter of Gilbert C. Trufant, of Bath.

CHILD:

135. I. Charles Marshall Scudder, born March 16, 1868; married Effie Haynes Richardson.+

68. HENRY BLATCHFORD SCUDDER [6] (Alicia H.,[5] Henry,[4] Samuel,[3] Henry,[2] Henry [1]), son of Alicia Harriet Blatchford and Charles William Scudder, was born June 18, 1844, at Brookline, Massachusetts; married April 20, 1866, at Andover, Massachusetts, Julia Randolph Perry, born April 29, 1843, at Boston, Massachusetts, daughter of Oliver Hazard Perry of Andover, Massachusetts, and Elizabeth Ann Randolph.

CHILDREN:

136. I. Mary Moseley Scudder, born April 21, 1867, at Needham, Mass.

137. II. Marshall Sears Scudder, born May 9, 1870; married Anna Behrmann Meyer.+

138. III. Alice Blatchford Scudder, born June 5, 1872, at Needham, Mass.

139. IV. Anne Randolph Scudder, born Dec. 9, 1874, at Needham, Mass.; married Oct. 22, 1910, at North Yakima, Washington, Fidelio King Hiscock, son of Hon. Frank Hiscock, of Syracuse, N. Y.

140. V. Lucy Randolph Scudder, born June 4, 1877, at Needham, Mass.

141.   VI.   Bessie Perry Scudder, born Aug. 26, 1879; married Charles A. Marsh.

142.   VII.   Randolph Perry Scudder, born Aug. 31, 1885, at Brookline, Mass.; married May 12, 1909, at North Yakima, Washington, Marjorie Fairchild Moran, daughter of Harry Fairchild Moran.

69. WINTHROP SALSTONSTALL SCUDDER [6] (Alicia H.,[5] Henry,[4] Samuel,[3] Henry,[2] Henry [1]), son of Alicia Harriet Blatchford and Charles William Scudder, was born July 26, 1847, at Brookline, Massachusetts; married first, April 11, 1888, at Albany, New York, Caroline Augusta Townsend, born October 18, 1854, at Albany, New York, died July 10, 1889, at Brookline, Massachusetts, daughter of Theodore Townsend, Esq., of Albany; married second, June 25, 1901, at Cambridge, Massachusetts, Jeanette Sumner Markham, born January 1, 1862, at Coldwater, Michigan, daughter of Edward Willoughby Markham, of Coldwater.

CHILD:

143.   I.   Theodore Townsend Scudder, born July 3, 1889, at Brookline, Mass.; married June 15, 1911, Carolyn Sturgis, born June 16, 1891, daughter of Russell Sturgis, Jr., and Anne Outram (Bangs) Sturgis.

72. AMY BLATCHFORD [6] (Thomas W.,[5] Thomas W.,[4] Samuel,[3] Henry,[2] Henry [1]), daughter of Thomas Wickes Blatchford and Jane Bunce Smith, was born September 4, 1855, at Great Barrington, Massachusetts; married June 9, 1883, at Brooklyn, New York, Samuel Dwight Wilcox, born May 6, 1862, at Ithaca, New York, died August 25, 1909, at New York City, son of Samuel Halliday Wilcox of Ithaca, New York.

CHILD:

144   I.   Thomas Blatchford Wilcox, born May 27, 1885, at New Brighton, Staten Island, N. Y.

75. THOMAS WINDEATT BLATCHFORD [6] (Samuel,[5] Thomas W.,[4] Samuel,[3] Henry,[2] Henry [1]), son of Samuel Blatchford

E. W. Blatchford,
May, 31, 1912.

and Agnes Euphemia Leadbeater, was born January 24, 1857,
at New York City; married November 23, 1881, at Chicago,
Illinois, Susie Carter, born January 7, 1863, at Chicago, died
January 5, 1900, at Chicago, daughter of Abile Harrison
Carter, of Chicago.

CHILD:

145.   I.   Carter Blatchford, born Nov. 26, 1882, at Chicago;
             married August 30, 1906, at Milwaukee, Wis.,
             Ivy Tichenor, born Dec. 25, 1887, at Oakland,
             Cal., daughter of Col. Anson Tichenor, of New
             York City.

76. RICHARD MILFORD BLATCHFORD [6] (Samuel,[5] Thomas
W.,[4] Samuel,[3] Henry,[2] Henry[1]), son of Samuel Blatchford
and Agnes Euphemia Leadbeater, was born August 7, 1859,
at Fort Hamilton, Long Island, New York; profession, Lieu-
tenant Colonel, U. S. A.; married July 27, 1887, at Brooklyn,
New York, Natalie Cary Green, born July 25, 1864, at Middletown, Delaware, daughter of Sewell Green, Esq., of Middletown. No children.

79. HENRY COMAN HOPKINS [6] (Alicia H.,[5] Samuel M.,[4]
Samuel,[3] Henry,[2] Henry [1]), son of Alicia Harriet Blatchford
and Nathaniel Fuller Hopkins, was born May 2, 1845, at New
York; married October 10, 1872, at Brooklyn, New York,
Susan Wells Kent, born January 20, 1846, at Brooklyn, New
York, died May 18, 1910, at Brooklyn, New York, daughter of
Henry Augustus Kent, Esq., of Brooklyn.

CHILDREN:

146.   I.   Henry Kent Hopkins, born Aug. 16, 1873; mar-
             ried Louise Amelia de Gard.+
147.   II.   Gerald Wells Hopkins, born Oct. 3, 1875; mar-
             ried Georgianna Washington Grunthol.+
148.   III. Ethel Hopkins, born Nov. 28, 1881, at Brooklyn,
             New York.

82. NATHANIEL FULLER HOPKINS [6] (Alicia H.,[5] Samuel
M.,[4] Samuel,[3] Henry,[2] Henry [1]), son of Alicia Harriet Blatch-

ford and Nathaniel Fuller Hopkins, was born September 10, 1851, at New York City; married first, August, 1875, at Des Moines, Iowa, Caroline Adams, born May, 1858, at Boone, Iowa, daughter of Peter Adams of Boone (divorced); married second, June 24, 1888, at New York City, Clara Appel, born April 23, 1873, daughter of Adam Appel, of Chicago.

CHILDREN:

149.   I.   Alicia Harriet Hopkins, born Oct. 23, 1875, at Des Moines, Iowa; died Dec. 22, 1885, at Chicago, Ill.

150.   II.   Samuel Milford Hopkins, born May 17, 1879, at Savanna, Ill.; died Dec. 29, 1885, at Chicago.

151.   III.   Samuel Blatchford Hopkins, born August, 1886, at Chicago; died February, 1887, at Chicago.

152.   IV.   Barbara Amy Hopkins, born Feb. 12, 1893, at New York City; died May 17, 1910, at Brooklyn, N. Y.

83. RICHARD MILFORD BLATCHFORD[6] (Henry S.,[5] Samuel M.,[4] Samuel,[3] Henry,[2] Henry[1]), son of Henry Samuel Blatchford and Martha Crossman, was born June 12, 1845, at Cincinnati, Ohio; died January 5, 1891, at Fronard, France; married in 1872, at Baden Baden, Germany, Amelie Kancher, born at Baden Baden, Germany, daughter of Dr. Frederick Kancher, of Baden Baden.

CHILDREN:

153.   I.   Henriette Blatchford, born Feb. 10, 1874; married Edward Schiffmacher.+

154.   II.   Cecil Blatchford, born in 1876, at Baden Baden, Germany; died in 1876, an infant of a few weeks.

155.   III.   Pierre Blatchford, born June 22, 1878, at Baden Baden, Germany.

84. HELEN ALICIA THERESE BLATCHFORD[6] (Henry S.,[5] Samuel M.,[4] Samuel,[3] Henry,[2] Henry[1]), daughter of Henry Samuel Blatchford and Martha Crossman, was born November 27, 1849, at Cincinnati, Ohio; married October 7, 1873, at

Carlsruhe, Germany, Charles Rule, born March 9, 1850, at
Cincinnati, Ohio, died August 30, 1885, at Branch Hill, Ohio,
son of Charles Rule, Esq., of Cincinnati.

CHILDREN:

156.   I. Blatchford Rule, born Nov. 3, 1874, at Branch
          Hill, O.; died Nov. 5, 1874, at Branch Hill.
157. II. Vladimir Blatchford Rule, born May 30, 1877;
          married Lillian Claire Hartman.+
158. III. Beverly Charles Rule, born March 27, 1881, at
          Branch Hill, O.

89. SAMUEL APPLETON BLATCHFORD [6] (Samuel,[5] Richard
M.,[4] Samuel[3] Henry,[2] Henry[1]), son of Samuel Blatchford
and Caroline Frances Appleton, was born September 9, 1845,
at Hell Gate, New York; died October 22, 1905, at New York
City; married June 10, 1869, Wilhelmina Bogart Conger, born
April 11, 1848, at Grassy Point, Rockland County, New York,
daughter of Abraham B. Conger, Esq., of Waldberg, Rockland
County, New York. Counsellor at Law; "Standing Master in
Chancery and Examiner, United States Circuit Court, South-
ern District of New York." No children.

90. JULIAN POTTER [6] (Julia M.,[5] Richard M.,[4] Samuel,[3]
Henry,[2] Henry[1]), son of Julia Maria Blatchford and Edward
Tuckerman Potter, was born August 10, 1858, at New Ro-
chelle, New York; married September 14, 1894, at Pittsburg,
Pennsylvania, Alice Pixley, born May 14, 1873, at Portland,
Oregon, daughter of Enoch Pixley, of San Francisco, Cali-
fornia, and Anne Shea.

CHILD:

159.   I. Julia Anne Dorothea Potter, born Oct. 24, 1905, at
          Nassau, N. P., Bahamas.

91. ETHELINDA POTTER [6] (Julia M.,[5] Richard M.,[4] Samuel,[3] Henry,[2] Henry[1]), daughter of Julia Maria Blatchford
and Edward Tuckerman Potter, was born November 20, 1860,
at Philadelphia, Pennsylvania; married May 9, 1883, at New
York City, Howard Nott Potter, born May 6, 1859, at New

York City, son of Clarkson Nott Potter, Esq., of New York City, and Virginia Mitchell.

CHILDREN:

160. I. Howard Clarkson Potter, born Nov. 30, 1894, at Paris, France; died Dec. 25, 1894, at Paris.

161. II. John Howard Nott Potter, born Sept. 20, 1896, at New Rochelle, N. Y.

162. III. Ethel Julia Howard Potter, born Jan. 3, 1898, at New Rochelle, N. Y.

92. EDWARD CLARKSON POTTER [6] (Julia M.,[5] Richard M.,[4] Samuel,[3] Henry,[2] Henry [1]), son of Julia Maria Blatchford and Edward Tuckerman Potter, was born August 11, 1862, at New York City; married January 15, 1885, at Villa d'Anglade, Pau, France, Emily Blanche Havemeyer, born September 12, 1866, at New York City, daughter of Theodore Augustus Havemeyer, Esq., of New York City.

CHILDREN:

163. I. Edward Clarkson Potter, born Dec. 19, 1885; married Lisa Bingham Marshall.+

164. II. Dorothea Havemeyer Potter, born Aug. 23, 1887; married William Gordon Coogan.+

165. III. Emily de Loosey Potter, born Aug. 9, 1889, at Newport, R. I.; married Sept. 21, 1911, at Clearview, Westchester, N. Y., Charles Havemeyer Jackson.

166. IV. Thomas Windeatt Potter, born May 14, 1891, at Westchester, N. Y.

167. V. Maria Blanche Potter, born June 29, 1892, at Westchester.

168. VI. Theodore Havemeyer Potter, born Sept. 5, 1893, at Westchester.

169. VII. Charles Robert Potter, born May 7, 1895, at Westchester.

170. VIII. Julia Blatchford Potter, born Oct. 18, 1896, at Westchester.

171. IX. Lillian Frederika Potter, born Jan. 23, 1899, at Westchester.

172.   X. Richard Milford Blatchford Potter, born Sept.
               2, 1900, at Westchester.
173.   XI. Eleanor Mary Potter, born July 18, 1902, at
               Westchester.

95. Louisa Millicent Windeatt Potter [6] (Julia M.,[5]
Richard M.,[4] Samuel,[3] Henry,[2] Henry [1]), daughter of Julia
Maria Blatchford and Edward Tuckerman Potter, was born
February 7, 1872, at Newport, Rhode Island; married first,
April 19, 1902, at Newport, Rhode Island, Joseph Earl Shef-
field, born November 16, 1871, at Attleboro, Massachusetts,
died October 16, 1903, at New York City, son of George St.
John Sheffield, Esq., of Attleboro. She married second, May
23, 1907, at New York City, William Adams Delano, born
Jan. 21, 1872, at New York, son of Eugene Delano, of New
York.

CHILD:

174.   I. William Richard Potter Delano, born July 31, 1909.

96. Julia Selden Potter [6] (Julia M.,[5] Richard M.,[4] Samuel,[3] Henry,[2] Henry [1]), daughter of Julia Maria Blatchford
and Edward Tuckerman Potter, was born July 29, 1875, at
Newport, Rhode Island; married Sept. 12, 1905, at Goring on
Thames, England, Tompkins McIlvaine, son of Reed McIlvaine, Esq., of New York City, and Lena Tompkins.

CHILDREN:

175.   I. Alexander McIlvaine, born Sept. 1, 1910.
175½. Julia Dorothea McIlvaine, born May 12, 1912, at
               New York.

97. Paul Blatchford [6] (Eliphalet W.,[5] John,[4] Samuel,[3]
Henry,[2] Henry [1]), son of Eliphalet Wickes Blatchford and
Mary Emily Williams, was born July 18, 1859, at Chicago, Illi-
nois; married May 24, 1887, at Bangor, Maine, Frances Veazie
Lord, born April 22, 1866, at Bangor, Maine, daughter of
Charles Veazie Lord, of Bangor, and Frances Elizabeth
Strickland.

CHILDREN:

176.   I.   John Blatchford, born April 20, 1888, at Oak
                Park, Ill.
177.   II.   Dorothy Lord Blatchford, born Dec. 10, 1889, at
                Oak Park, Ill.
178.   III.   Barbara Blatchford, born Sept. 14, 1894, at Oak
                Park, Ill.
179.   IV.   Charles Lord Blatchford, born Feb. 12, 1897, at
                Plasderwa, Oak Park, Ill.

98. AMY BLATCHFORD [6] (Eliphalet W.,[5] John,[4] Samuel,[3] Henry,[2] Henry [1]), daughter of Eliphalet Wickes Blatchford and Mary Emily Williams, was born May 20, 1862, at Chicago, Illinois; married November 7, 1889, at Chicago, Rev. Howard Sweetser Bliss, D. D., of Brooklyn, New York, born December 6, 1860, at Suk-el-Ghurb, on Mount Lebanon, near Beirût, Syria, son of Rev. Daniel Bliss, D. D., of Beirût, Syria, and Abby Wood.

CHILDREN:

180.   I.   Mary Williams Bliss, born Nov. 16, 1890, at
                Brooklyn, N. Y.
181.   II.   Margaret Blatchford Bliss, born Jan. 21, 1893, at
                Brooklyn, N. Y.
182.   III.   Alice Wood Bliss, born Nov. 23, 1894, at Upper
                Montclair, N. J.
183.   IV.   Daniel Bliss, II, born March 15, 1898, at Upper
                Montclair, N. J.
184.   V.   Howard Huntington Bliss, born April 12, 1903,
                at Beirût, Syria.

102. CHARLES HAMMOND BLATCHFORD [6] (Eliphalet W.,[5] John,[4] Samuel,[3] Henry,[2] Henry [1]), son of Eliphalet Wickes Blatchford and Mary Emily Williams, was born January 2, 1874, at Evanston, Illinois; married November 30, 1899, at New Haven, Connecticut, Carita Tyler Clark, born July 6, 1869, at Newton Centre, Massachusetts, daughter of Charles Peter Clark, of New Haven (died in Nice, France, March 21, 1901), and Caroline Tyler (died in Brookline, Massachusetts, June 22, 1906).

CHILDREN:

185.   I.   Eliphalet Lawrence Blatchford, born May 3,
             1902, at Chicago, Ill.
186.   II.   Charles Hammond Blatchford, Jr., born May 31,
             1904, at Ulmenheim, Chicago, Ill.
187. III.   Huntington Blatchford, born Nov. 18, 1907, at
             Winnetka, Ill.

104. JOHN BLATCHFORD COLLINS⁶ (Martha W.,⁵ John,⁴
Samuel,³ Henry,² Henry¹), son of Martha Wickes Blatchford
and Morris Collins, was born September 7, 1853, at Hazeldean,
near Quincy, Illinois; married November 11, 1874, at St.
Louis, Missouri, Nellie Davis, born February 21, 1854, at Cincinnati, Ohio, daughter of Cornelius Edmund Davis, of St.
Louis (divorced); married second, December 15, 1897, at
Miles City, Montana, Nellie Rebecca Thompson, born February 18, 1874, near Dwight, Illinois, died June 18, 1903, at
Forsyth, Montana, daughter of Thomas Jefferson Thompson,
of Forsyth, Montana.

CHILDREN:

188.   I.   Morris Collins, born Oct. 26, 1875, at St. Louis,
             Mo.; died July 21, 1894, at St. Louis.
189.   II.   Charles Blatchford Collins, born Oct. 23, 1877;
             married Helen Klein.+

107. AMOS MORRIS COLLINS⁶ (Martha W.,⁵ John,⁴ Samuel,³ Henry,² Henry¹), son of Martha Wickes Blatchford and
Morris Collins, was born November 25, 1857, at St. Louis, Missouri; died January 26, 1902, at Chicago, Illinois; married
February 5, 1879, at Creston, Iowa, Charlotte Brown Young,
born October 28, 1862, near Princeton, Illinois, daughter of
Joseph Rogers Young, of Creston, Iowa.

CHILDREN:

190.   I.   Martha Wickes Collins, born Dec. 25, 1880, at
             Orient, Iowa; died March 11, 1881, at Orient.
191.   II.   Anna Blatchford Collins, born Sept. 2, 1892, at
             Battle Creek, Michigan.

192. III. Amos Morris Collins, born March 27, 1900, at Chicago, Ill.

108. MARTHA BLATCHFORD COLLINS [6] (Martha W.,[5] John,[4] Samuel,[3] Henry,[2] Henry [1]), daughter of Martha Wickes Blatchford and Morris Collins, was born July 12, 1859, at St. Louis, Missouri; died November 6, 1889, at Kansas City, Missouri; married May 26, 1881, at Jacksonville Illinois, John Franklin Downing, born August 24, 1854, at Virginia, Illinois, son of Daniel Rice Downing of Virginia, Illinois.

CHILDREN:

193. I. Frank Collins Downing, born Feb. 19, 1884, at Kansas City, Missouri.

194. II. Blatchford Downing, born Dec. 10, 1885, at Kansas City, Mo.

112. FRANCIS WICKES BLATCHFORD [6] (Nathaniel H.,[5] John,[4] Samuel,[3] Henry,[2] Henry [1]), son of Nathaniel Hopkins Blatchford and Ella Marion Philbrick, was born September 20, 1875, at Chicago, Illinois; married November 29, 1902, at Blair Lodge, Lake Forest, Illinois, Frances Greene Larned, born October 17, 1879, at Chicago, daughter of Walter Cranston Larned, Esq., of Lake Forest, Illinois.

CHILDREN:

195. I. Ella Marion Blatchford, born Nov. 5, 1903, at Chicago.

196. II. Elsie Larned Blatchford, born Nov. 21, 1905, at Chicago.

197. III. Francis Wickes Blatchford, Jr., born Oct. 27, 1908, at Winnetka, Ill.

198. IV. Walter Larned Blatchford, born April 15, 1910, at Winnetka.

116. KATE DALLAS WATSON [6] (Mary J.,[5] Frederick,[4] Samuel,[3] Henry,[2] Henry [1]), daughter of Mary Jane Blatchford and William Berger Watson, was born February 14, 1872, at Hannibal, Missouri; married June 27, 1901, at Paia, Maui, Hawaiian Islands, William Joseph Forbes, born October 8,

1866, at Honolulu, Hawaiian Islands, son of Anderson Oliver Forbes, of Honolulu.

CHILDREN:

199.   I.   Theodore Watson Forbes, born May 21, 1902, at Honolulu, H. I.
200.   II.   Frederick Blatchford Forbes, born Jan. 23, 1904, at Honolulu, H. I.
201.   III. Marion Chamberlain Forbes, born July 1, 1905, at Honolulu, H. I.
202.   IV.   Frances Alicia Forbes, born Sept. 15, 1908, at Honolulu, H. I.
203.   V.   Katharine Wilhelmina Forbes, born Jan. 4, 1911.

118. ANNIE MORRIS WILBUR [6] (Almira,[5] Frederick,[4] Samuel,[3] Henry,[2] Henry [1]), daughter of Almira Blatchford and Thomas Wilbur, was born May 21, 1869, at Ralls, Missouri; married April 12, 1891, at Gunnison, Colorado, Wilbur Truman Liggett, M. D., born November 26, 1866, at Marysville, Ohio, son of William Liggett, of Xenia, Ohio. No children.

120. LOUISA BRIGGS WILBUR [6] (Almira,[5] Frederick,[4] Samuel,[3] Henry,[2] Henry [1]), daughter of Almira Blatchford and Thomas Wilbur, was born September 18, 1874, at Hannibal, Missouri; married May 22, 1893, at Pitkin, Gunnison County, Colorado, Garritt Benton Hudnutt, born February 22, 1870, at Fort Madison, Iowa, son of David Benton Hudnutt of Fort Madison.

CHILDREN:

204.   I.   Thelma Fredda Hudnutt, born Feb. 4, 1895, at Cripple Creek, Colorado; died Dec. 27, 1899, at Colorado Springs, Colo.
205.   II.   Mina Edna Hudnutt, born Oct. 12, 1896, at Pitkin, Colo.
206.   III. Almira Anna Hudnutt, born Nov. 20, 1900, at Denver, Colo.

121. ALLIE MORRISS [6] (Sarah J.,[5] Frederick,[4] Samuel,[3] Henry,[2] Henry [1]), daughter of Sarah Julia Blatchford and

William Henry Harrison Morriss, was born October 17, 1868, at Steffenville, Missouri; married at "Hawthorne Home" (her father's residence), Shelby County, Missouri, James Edgar Day, born Oct. 30, 1852, at Lagrange, Missouri, son of William Gibson Day, of Lagrange, Missouri.

CHILDREN:

207. I. William Eliphalet Day, born July 1, 1894, at Lagrange, Mo.

208. II. Edgar Leonidas Day, born Aug. 26, 1896, at Epworth, Mo.; died May 21, 1908, at Bethel, Mo.

209. III. John Wilbur Day, born Nov. 23, 1897, at Epworth, Mo.

210. IV. Susan Lucile Day, born Feb. 25, 1899, at Sigsbee, Mo.

211. V. Grace Ellen Day, born April 4, 1900, at Sigsbee, Mo.

212 VI. Alfred Sylvester Day, born March 30, 1905, at Bethel, Mo.

213. VII. Sadie Viola Day, born Sept. 3, 1908, at Bethel, Mo.

122. EDWIN WILBUR MORRISS [6] (Sarah J.,[5] Frederick,[4] Samuel,[3] Henry,[2] Henry[1]), son of Sarah Julia Blatchford and William Henry Harrison Morriss, was born February 8, 1871, in Shelby County, Missouri; married January 1, 1896, at Lagrange, Lewis County, Missouri, Lydia Frances Courtney; born September 12, 1874, in Lewis County, Missouri, daughter of Marshal Mortimer Courtney, of Lagrange.

CHILDREN:

214. I. Noble Courtney Morriss, born Feb. 18, 1897, at Elgin, Mo.

215. II. Gwennola Blanche Morriss, born Aug. 30, 1898, at Lewistown, Mo.

216. III. Clara Marguerite Morriss, born July 31, 1902, at Ewing, Mo.

217. IV. Raymond Eliphalet Morriss, born Dec. 20, 1903, at Ewing, Mo.

218. V. Edna Frances Morriss, born Aug. 26, 1907, at Ewing, Mo.

123. ROSALIE MORRISS [6] (Sarah J.,[5] Frederick,[4] Samuel,[3] Henry,[2] Henry [1]), daughter of Sarah Julia Blatchford and William Henry Harrison Morriss, was born July 23, 1874, at "Hawthorne Home," Shelby County, Missouri; married February 15, 1900, at Milton Junction, Wisconsin, Reuben Delos Sprague, born August 17, 1877, at Milton, Wisconsin, son of Reuben Sprague of Milton.

CHILDREN:

219.   I.   Russell Glenn Sprague, born Aug. 8, 1905, at Crystal Falls, Mich.

220.   II.   Roland Delos Sprague, born July 21, 1911, at Bethel, Mo.

124. ANNA BELLE MORRISS [6] (Sarah J.,[5] Frederick,[4] Samuel,[3] Henry,[2] Henry [1]), daughter of Sarah Julia Blatchford and William Henry Harrison Morriss, was born August 20, 1876, at "Hawthorne Home," Shelby County, Missouri; married December 11, 1894, at "Hawthorne Home," Shelby County, Missouri, Harold Arthur Sprague, born October 19, 1874, at Otter Creek, Rock County, Wisconsin, son of Reuben Sprague of Milton, Wisconsin.

CHILDREN:

221.   I.   Paul Raymond Sprague, born Aug. 31, 1895, near "Hawthorne Home," Shelby Co., Mo.

222.   II.   Maurice Sprague, born Aug. 27, 1897, near "Hawthorne Home."

223.   III.   Vera Gladys Sprague, born Jan. 14, 1900, at Johnstown, Rock Co., Wis.

224.   IV.   Ralph Blatchford Sprague, born March 19, 1902, at Milton Junction, Wis.

225.   V.   Earl Edwin Sprague, born Oct. 28, 1904, at Beloit, Wis.

226.   VI.   Alta Grace Sprague, born Sept. 21, 1907, at Beloit.

227. VII.   Claude Milford Sprague, born Feb. 20, 1910, near Janesville, Wis.

125. FREDERICK BLATCHFORD MORRISS [6] (Sarah J.,[5] Frederick,[4] Samuel,[3] Henry,[2] Henry [1]), son of Sarah Julia Blatchford and William Henry Harrison Morriss, was born April 28, 1878, near Elgin, Missouri; married February 3, 1904, at Bethel, Missouri, Ida Marie Bower, born February 2, 1882, daughter of Walter Christopher Bower of Bethel, Missouri.

CHILDREN:

228.   I.   Harold Bower Morriss, born Dec. 17, 1905, at Green City, Mo.; died Jan. 31, 1906, at Green City.

229.   II.   Marie Kathryn Morriss, born Nov. 21, 1907, at Green City, Mo.

230.   III. Pauline Isabelle Morriss, born May 8, 1910, at Green City, Mo.

126. WILLIAM MILFORD MORRISS [6] (Sarah J.,[5] Frederick,[4] Samuel,[3] Henry,[2] Henry [1]), son of Sarah Julia Blatchford and William Henry Harrison Morriss, was born February 28, 1880, near Bethel, Missouri; married July 30, 1902, near Bethel, Missouri, Ada Lee Murray, born September 8, 1879, near Calhoun, Missouri, daughter of James Cornelius Murray, of near Bethel, Missouri.

CHILDREN:

231.   I.   Lee Milford Morriss, born Nov. 17, 1905, near Bethel, Mo.

232.   II.   Clara Irene Morriss, born Aug. 30, 1910, near Bethel, Mo.

SEVENTH GENERATION

135. CHARLES MARSHALL SCUDDER [7] (Francis H.,[6] Alicia H.,[5] Henry,[4] Samuel,[3] Henry,[2] Henry [1]), son of Francis Henry Scudder and Sarah Rollins Trufant, was born March 16, 1868, at Boston, Massachusetts; married January 1, 1891, at Brookline, Massachusetts, Effie Haynes Richardson, born August 18, 1870, at Brookline, Massachusetts, daughter of George Prentiss Richardson, of Brookline.

CHILDREN:

233.   I.   Margaret Francis Scudder, born Dec. 23, 1891, at Newton Centre, Mass.

234.   II.   Winthrop Richardson Scudder, born March 3, 1893, at Newton Highlands, Mass.

235.   III.   Dorothy Blatchford Scudder, born Sept. 23, 1895, at Needham, Mass.

236.   IV.   Gwendolyn Scudder, born Feb. 27, 1908, at Hingham, Mass.

137. MARSHALL SEARS SCUDDER [7] (Henry B.,[6] Alicia H.,[5] Henry,[4] Samuel,[3] Henry,[2] Henry [1]), son of Henry Blatchford Scudder and Julia Randolph Perry, was born May 9, 1870, at Needham, Massachusetts; married November 6, 1901, at North Yakima, Washington, Anna Behrmann Meyer, born October 5, 1873, at Stockton, California, daughter of Henry W. Meyer, of North Yakima.

CHILD:

237.   I.   Alice Behrmann Scudder, born March 27, 1904, at North Yakima.

146. HENRY KENT HOPKINS [7] (Henry C.,[6] Alicia H.,[5] Samuel M.,[4] Samuel,[3] Henry,[2] Henry [1]), son of Henry Coman Hopkins and Susan Wells Kent, was born August 16, 1873, at

Brooklyn, New York; married August 23, 1899, at Brooklyn, New York, Louise Amelia de Gard, born August 11, 1870, at Brooklyn, New York, died May 18, 1910, at Brooklyn, daughter of Maurice de Gard, of Staten Island, New York.

CHILD:

238.   I.   Henry Kent Hopkins, Jr., born Oct. 15, 1900, at Brooklyn, N. Y.

147. GERALD WELLS HOPKINS [7] (Henry C.,[6] Alicia H.,[5] Samuel M.,[4] Samuel,[3] Henry,[2] Henry [1]), son of Henry Coman Hopkins and Susan Wells Kent, was born October 3, 1875, at Brooklyn, New York; married August 21, 1900, at Brooklyn, Georgianna Washington Grunthol, born February 22, 1872, at New York City, daughter of George Grunthol, of Brooklyn.

153. HENRIETTE BLATCHFORD [7] (Richard M.,[6] Henry S.,[5] Samuel M.,[4] Samuel,[3] Henry,[2] Henry [1]), daughter of Richard Milford Blatchford and Amelie Kancher, was born February 10, 1874, at New York City; married April 26, 1892, at Nancy, France, Edward Schiffmacher, born at Paris, France, son of General Edward Schiffmacher of the Prussian Army, of Berlin, Germany.

157. VLADIMIR BLATCHFORD RULE [7] (Helen A. T.,[6] Henry S.,[5] Samuel M.,[4] Samuel,[3] Henry,[2] Henry [1]), son of Helen Alicia Therese Blatchford and Charles Rule, was born May 30, 1877, at Branch Hill, Ohio; married June 15, 1898, at Hamilton, Ohio, Lillian Claire Hartman, born October 23, 1880, at Walnut Hills, daughter of William Hartman, Esq., of Cincinnati, Ohio.

CHILDREN:

239.   I.   Beverly Blatchford Rule, born March 23, 1899, at Cincinnati, O.

240.   II.   Ralph Milford Blatchford Rule, born Dec. 24, 1901, at Linwood, O.

163. EDWARD CLARKSON POTTER, JR.[7] (Edward C.,[6] Julia M.,[5] Richard M.,[4] Samuel,[3] Henry,[2] Henry [1]), son of Edward

Clarkson Potter and Emily Blanche Havemeyer, was born December 19, 1885, at New York City; married January 14, 1905,
at New York City, Lisa Bingham Marshall, daughter of S.
Duncan Marshall, of New York.

CHILDREN:

241.   I.   Katharine Marshall Potter, born May 17, 1906, at
            Cambridge, Mass.
242. II.   Edward Clarkson Potter, III, born Dec. 3, 1909, at
            Woodmere, Long Island.

164. DOROTHEA HAVEMEYER POTTER [7] (Edward C.,[6] Julia
M.,[5] Richard M.,[4] Samuel,[3] Henry,[2] Henry [1]), daughter of Edward Clarkson Potter and Emily Blanche Havemeyer, was
born August 23, 1887, at Newport, Rhode Island; married December 18, 1907, at New York City, William Gordon Coogan,
son of James G. Coogan, of New York.

CHILDREN:

243.   I.   William Gordon Coogan, Jr., born June 24, 1908,
            at Ottersham, England.
244. II.   Theodore Havemeyer Coogan, born August 28,
            1909, at Newport, R. I.
245. III.   Emily Maria Coogan, born June 29, 1911, at Pel-
            ham Manor, N. Y.

189. CHARLES BLATCHFORD COLLINS [7] (John B.,[6] Martha
W.,[5] John,[4] Samuel,[3] Henry,[2] Henry [1]), son of John Blatch-
ford Collins and Nellie Davis, was born October 23, 1877, at
St. Louis, Missouri; married June 21, 1905, at St. Louis, Helen
Klein, born October 8, 1878, at St. Louis, daughter of Judge
Jacob Klein, of St. Louis; by profession, a lawyer.

CHILD:

246.   I.   Charles Klein Collins, born Dec. 20, 1910, at St.
            Louis, Mo.

APPENDIX A

HEATH FAMILY

ROBERT HEATH, in his will dated January 22, 1779, styled himself "Robert Heath, of Totnes, in the County of Devon, Blacksmith." With other bequests he specified, "Also I give unto my daughter Mary, my *Silver quart cup*." He married first, June 10, 1733, Mary Alford [the Totnes Registry being simply, "Robert Heath and Mary Alford, both of this town"]; married second, Susanna ——————.

CHILDREN:

By first marriage:

I. Mary Heath, born in 1735; married Henry Blatchford.+

II. Sarah Heath, baptized Sept. 21, 1737, at Totnes, Devonshire, England.

III. Susanna Heath, baptized Aug. 15, 1739, at Totnes; married Richard Roe, of Dartmouth, Devonshire, to whom her father bequeathed his "silver pint cup."

IV. Robert Heath, baptized June 17, 1741, at Totnes.

V. Samuel Heath, baptized Nov. 1, 1744, at Totnes.

VI. Richard Heath, baptized June 18, 1746, at Totnes.

VII. Henry Heath.

VIII. William Heath.

IX. Jane Heath, baptized May 19, 1748, at Totnes.

X. Jane Heath, baptized Nov. 22, 1749, at Totnes; married shortly after her father's death, —————— Goldsworthy.

By second marriage:

XI. John Heath, to whom he bequeathed the house and garden in Totnes after his mother's death. He died at Gravesend, on the Thames, below London, without issue.

101

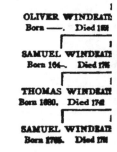

OLIVER WINDEATE
Born ——.   Died 18

SAMUEL WINDEATE
Born 164—   Died 17

THOMAS WINDEATE
Born 1680.   Died 174

SAMUEL WINDEATE
Born 1705.   Died 17

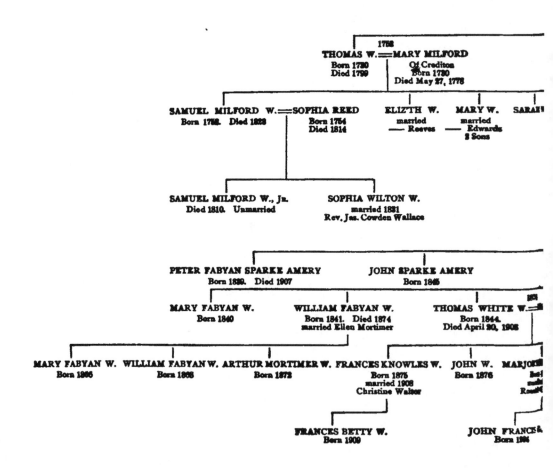

1752
THOMAS W.══MARY MILFORD
Born 1730   Of Crediton
Died 1799   Born 1730
                   Died May 27, 1776

SAMUEL MILFORD W.══SOPHIA REED   ELIZ'TH W.   MARY W.   SARAH
Born 1752.   Died 1822   Born 1754   married   married
                           Died 1814   —— Reeves   Edwards
                                                               2 Sons

SAMUEL MILFORD W., Jr.   SOPHIA WILTON W.
Died 1810.   Unmarried   married 1831
                                 Rev. Jas. Cowden Wallace

PETER FABYAN SPARKE AMERY   JOHN SPARKE AMERY
Born 1839.   Died 1907   Born 1845

MARY FABYAN W.   WILLIAM FABYAN W.   THOMAS WHITE W.══
Born 1840   Born 1841. Died 1874   Born 1844.
                        married Ellen Mortimer   Died April 20, 1908

MARY FABYAN W.   WILLIAM FABYAN W.   ARTHUR MORTIMER W.   FRANCES KNOWLES W.   JOHN W.   MARJOR
Born 1906   Born 1908   Born 1872   Born 1875   Born 1876
                                                             married 1908
                                                             Christine Walter

FRANCES BETTY W.   JOHN FRANCIS
Born 1909   Born 19

IX B

WINDEATT FAMILY

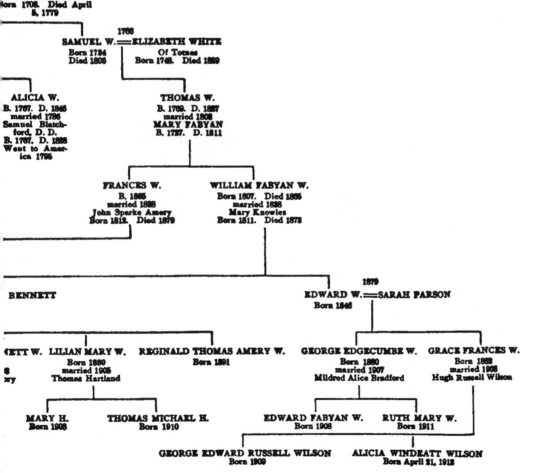

CHRISTIAN SNOW

MARY HALWELL
Born ——. Died 1711

MARY WATSON
Born ——. Died 1719

SARAH EDGECUMBE
(Related to Lord Mount
Edgecumbe)
of Edgecumbe
near Milton Abbott
Born 1708. Died April
5, 1779

1766
SAMUEL W.══ELIZABETH WHITE
Born 1734   Of Totnes
Died 1806   Born 1748. Died 1829

ALICIA W.
B. 1767. D. 1946
married 1786
Samuel Blatch-
ford, D. D.
B. 1767. D. 1828
Went to Amer-
ica 1795

THOMAS W.
B. 1769. D. 1827
married 1803
MARY FABYAN
B. 1727. D. 1811

FRANCES W.
B. 1805
married 1838
John Sparke Amery
Born 1812. Died 1879

WILLIAM FABYAN W.
Born 1807. Died 1855
married 1838
Mary Knowles
Born 1811. Died 1873

1879
BENNETT   EDWARD W.══SARAH PARSON
Born 1846

BENNETT W.   LILIAN MARY W.   REGINALD THOMAS AMERY W.   GEORGE EDGECUMBE W.   GRACE FRANCES W.
             Born 1880   Born 1891   Born 1880   Born 1882
Mary   married 1905   married 1907   married 1906
             Thomas Hartland   Mildred Alice Bradford   Hugh Russell Wilson

        MARY H.   THOMAS MICHAEL H.   EDWARD FABYAN W.   RUTH MARY W.
        Born 1906   Born 1910   Born 1908   Born 1911

            GEORGE EDWARD RUSSELL WILSON   ALICIA WINDEATT WILSON
                    Born 1909   Born April 21, 1912

SAMUEL WINDEATT,
Of Totnes, Devonshire, 1703-1794

EXTRACTS FROM WILL

OF

SAMUEL WINDEATT.

EXTRACTED FROM THE DISTRICT REGISTRY ATTACHED TO THE
PROBATE DIVISION OF HER MAJESTY'S HIGH COURT
OF JUSTICE AT EXETER.

"In the Name of God Amen I Samuel Windeatt of Berry
Pomeroy in the County of Devon Gentleman being in good
health and of a sound and perfect mind memory and understanding thanks be to Almighty God for the same but con-
sidering the uncertainty of this transitory life do make and
publish this my last Will and Testament in manner following
(that is to say) First I recommend my soul into the hands of
Almighty God who gave it in an humble hope that he will
receive the same into his favour in and through the merits of
his dear Son and our most blessed Redeemer Jesus Christ and
my body to be decently buried at the discretion of my Executor hereinafter named.

And as to my worldly state wherewith it hath pleased
God to bless me I give devise and dispose of the same as follows (to wit) First I give and devise unto my son Thomas
Windeatt and his assigns for and during the term of his nat-
ural life All that piece or parcel of land with the appurten-
ances situate and being in the Town of Modbury in the said
County of Devon on which there now is or formerly was a
dwelling house and from and after his decease I give and
devise the same unto my Grandson Samuel Milford Windeatt
(Son of the said Thomas Windeatt) his heirs and assigns for
ever. Also I give and bequeath unto my said grandson Samuel
Milford Windeatt All those my two leasehold messuages ten-
ements or dwelling houses called or commonly known by the
name of Manings House and the Bridge House together with

108

the quays and granaries which I now hold for the life of my said Son Thomas Windeatt all situate and being at Bridgetown within the parish of Berry Pomeroy aforesaid and now in the possession of John Cuming and others To hold the same unto the said Samuel Milford Windeatt his executors, administrators and assigns for and during all my right title interest term and terms of years therein now to come and unexpired Upon trust nevertheless and to and for the uses ends intents and purposes hereinafter mentioned (that is to say) Upon trust that he the said Samuel Milford Windeatt his executors and administrators shall and do from time to time demise set or let the said premises every or any part thereof at an yearly rent to any person or persons whomsoever and after reimbursing himself and themselves as well as all such sum and sums of money as he or they shall or may lay out expend or be put unto in the necessary repairs of the said premises and for the rates and taxes of the same as all such costs charges damages and expenses as he or they shall or may incur sustain or be put unto in or about the trust hereby in him and them reposed shall and do pay and apply the neat and clear rents issues and profits thereof in and towards the maintenance clothing and education of my Granddaughter Alice Windeatt (daughter of my said son Thomas Windeatt) until she shall attain the full age of twenty-one years.''

After the signing of his will Mr. Windeatt makes the following thoughtful, generous provision:

''Be it Remembered that I the above named Samuel Windeatt the testator do order and direct my son Samuel Windeatt my Executor above named to sign and execute to my said son Thomas Windeatt and to my four Granddaughters Elizabeth, Mary, Sarah and Alice Windeatt above named a good and sufficient release and discharge of all such sum and sums of money as they or any or either of them shall or may owe me on any account whatsoever at the time of my decease it being my Will and intention to acquit them from all claims and demands which shall or may be due and owing to me from them or any or either of them at that time And I do further order and direct that this shall be taken for part of my Will as fully to all intents and purposes as if written and inserted in the body thereof.''

HON. SAMUEL HUBBARD, L.L.D.
Justice of the Supreme Judicial Court of Massachusetts

APPENDIX C

HUBBARD FAMILY

1. SAMUEL HUBBARD, son of William Hubbard * and Joanna
Perkins, was born June 2, 1785, at Boston, Massachusetts; died
December 24, 1847, at Boston; married first, June 8, 1815,
Mary Ann Greene who died July 10, 1827, daughter of Gardiner Greene, merchant, of Boston; married second, October
28, 1828, Mary Ann (Coit) Blatchford, widow of Rev. Henry
Blatchford [No. 8], born January 21, 1798, at New York City,
died July 20, 1869, at Liverpool, England, daughter of Elisha
Coit, Esq., of New York City, and Rebecca Manwaring. Justice of the Supreme Judicial Court of Massachusetts; LL. D.,
both Yale, 1827, and Harvard, 1842.

CHILDREN:

2.　I.　Elizabeth Greene Hubbard, born Feb. 11, 1817;
married Edward Buck; died May 14, 1890.

3.　II.　Joanna Perkins Hubbard, born Sept. 26, 1818;
married Philo Augustus Gillett; died Aug. 4,
1862.

4.　III.　Mary Ann Hubbard, born Sept. 7, 1820; married
Edgecumbe Heath Blatchford. [No. 24.]

5.　IV.　Gardiner Greene Hubbard, born Aug. 25, 1822;
married Gertrude McCurdy; died Dec. 10,
1897.

6.　V.　Caroline Hubbard, born May 11, 1826; married
Theodore Frelinghuysen McCurdy; died Nov.
15, 1868.

---

* William Hubbard, born February 25, 1739, at New London, Connecticut, died April 3, 1801, at New York; married second, May 13,
1779, Joanna Perkins, born December 10, 1745, at Boston, died October
11, 1789, at Boston.

105

7. VI. Sarah Wisner Hubbard, born Aug. 16, 1829, at
Boston, Mass.; died Feb. 26, 1856, at Boston.

8. VII. Samuel Hubbard, born June 18, 1831; married
Sophie Hunt.+

9. VIII. Henry Blatchford Hubbard, born Jan. 8, 1833;
died Feb. 13, 1862, at Chicago, Ill.

10. IX. William Coit Hubbard, born Sept. 23, 1834; married Alice Frances Hammond.+

11. X. James Mascarene Hubbard, born Aug. 15, 1836;
married Sarah Hill Tomlinson.+

12. XI. Charles Eustis Hubbard, born Aug. 7, 1842; married Caroline Dennie Tracy.+

8. SAMUEL HUBBARD,[2] son of Samuel Hubbard and Mary
Ann (Coit) Blatchford, was born June 18, 1831, at Boston,
Massachusetts; died February 10, 1912, at Oakland, Cali-
fornia; married August 12, 1857, at San Francisco, Sophie
Hunt, born November 15, 1836, at New York City, daughter of
Jonathan Hunt, of Oakland, California.

CHILDREN:

14. I. Katharine Hubbard, born Dec. 28, 1858; married
John McEwen Hyde.+

15. II. Samuel Hubbard, Jr., born May 17, 1863; married
Josephine Wolfsberger.+

16. III. Mary Winthrop Hubbard, born Sept. 5, 1864; married William Donnison Swan.+

17. IV. William Babcock Hubbard, born June 19, 1867;
married Katharine Hayes Peck.+

18. V. Charles Parker Hubbard, born Jan. 26, 1871; married Georgie Mabel Strong.+

10. WILLIAM COIT HUBBARD,[2] son of Samuel Hubbard and
Mary Ann (Coit) Blatchford, was born September 23, 1834, at
Boston, Massachusetts; died January 3, 1865, at Chicago, Illinois; married May 21, 1857, at Chicago, Alice Frances Hammond, born May 21, 1836, at Detroit, Michigan, died at Chicago, daughter of Charles Goodrich Hammond, Esq., of Chicago.

CHILDREN:

19.   I.   William Hammond Hubbard, born March 5, 1858;
           married Susan Campbell Weare.+
20.   II. Henry Mascarene Hubbard, born Feb. 9, 1860; mar-
           ried Louisa Shipman.+

11. JAMES MASCARENE HUBBARD,[2] son of Samuel Hubbard
and Mary Ann (Coit) Blatchford, was born August 15, 1836,
at Boston, Massachusetts; married October 16, 1861, at New
Haven, Connecticut, Sarah Hill Tomlinson, born December 15,
1839, at New Haven, daughter of Henry Abraham Tomlinson,
of New Haven, and Maria Beers Ives, of New Haven.

CHILDREN:

21.   I.   Florence Mascarene Hubbard, born Nov. 27, 1864;
            married Robert Rantoul.+
22.   II.   Roberta Wolcott Hubbard, born March 23, 1869, at
            Wellesley Hills, Massachusetts; died May 11,
            1879, at Wellesley Hills.
23.   III. Paul Mascarene Hubbard, born Aug. 18, 1876, at
            Cambridge, Mass.; married Dec. 5, 1905, at Con-
            cord, N. H., Martha Hartley Coit, born at Va-
            lencia, Spain, daughter of Levi Howland Coit
            and Martha Frothingham Hartley.

12. CHARLES EUSTIS HUBBARD,[2] son of Samuel Hubbard and
Mary Ann (Coit) Blatchford, was born August 7, 1842, at
Boston, Massachusetts; married December 10, 1872, at Boston,
Caroline Dennie Tracy, born August 25, 1847, at Boston,
daughter of Frederic Uriah Tracy, Esq., of Boston.

CHILDREN:

24.   I.   Helen Hubbard, born Dec. 3, 1873, at Boston; died
            Oct. 6, 1874, at Boston.
25.   II.   Frederic Tracy Hubbard, born Sept. 28, 1875;
            married Mary Bessie Welling.+
26.   III. Gardiner Greene Hubbard, born April 19, 1878, at
            Boston; unmarried.

27. IV. Gertrude Hubbard, born Feb. 1, 1880; married Harry Buckle.+

14. KATHARINE HUBBARD ³ (Samuel,² Samuel ¹), daughter of Samuel Hubbard and Sophie Hunt, was born December 28, 1858, at San Francisco, California; married October 21, 1885, at Oakland, California, Captain John McEwen Hyde (U. S. A.), born November 2, 1841, at New York City, son of Joseph Hyde, of New York City. No children.

15. SAMUEL HUBBARD, JR.³ (Samuel,² Samuel ¹), son of Samuel Hubbard and Sophie Hunt, was born May 17, 1863, at San Francisco, California; married June 28, 1905, at Blackheath, London, England, Josephine Wolfsberger, daughter of Charles George Wolfsberger, of Eastnor, Blackheath, London.

CHILDREN:

28. I. Bessie Carola Hubbard, born May 20, 1906, at Oakland.
29. II. Gertrude Sophie Hubbard, born Dec. 6, 1907, at Oakland.

16. MARY WINTHROP HUBBARD ³ (Samuel,² Samuel ¹), daughter of Samuel Hubbard and Sophie Hunt, was born September 5, 1864, at San Francisco, California; died July 20, 1908; married April 30, 1890, at Oakland, California, Dr. William Donnison Swan, born January 1; 1859, at Kennebunk, Maine, son of Rev. William D. Swan, of Cambridge, Massachusetts.

CHILDREN:

30. I. Marian Hubbard Swan, born Feb. 22, 1891, at Cambridge, Mass.
31. II. William Donnison Swan, born Oct. 9, 1894, at Cambridge, Mass.

17. WILLIAM BABCOCK HUBBARD ³ (Samuel,² Samuel ¹), son of Samuel Hubbard and Sophie Hunt, was born June 19, 1867, at Oakland, California; married March 26, 1901, at Milwaukee,

Wisconsin, Katharine Hayes Peck, born March 30, 1872, at Milwaukee, daughter of James Sydney Peck, of Milwaukee.

CHILDREN:

32.   I.   Katharine Hubbard, born June 13, 1905, at Oakland.
33.   II. Marjorie Hubbard, born June 29, 1907, at Milwaukee, Wis.
34.   III. Samuel Hubbard, born June 14, 1909, at Bellingham, Washington.

18. CHARLES PARKER HUBBARD [3] (Samuel,[2] Samuel [1]), son of Samuel Hubbard and Sophie Hunt, was born January 26, 1871, at San Francisco, California; married January 20, 1909, at Oakland, California, Georgie Mabel Strong, daughter of George H. Strong, of Oakland.

19. WILLIAM HAMMOND HUBBARD [3] (William C.,[2] Samuel [1]), son of William Coit Hubbard and Alice Frances Hammond, was born March 5, 1858, at Chicago, Illinois; died June 1, 1908, at Lake Forest, Illinois; married October 15, 1884, at Cedar Rapids, Iowa, Susan Campbell Weare, born April 9, 1863, at Cedar Rapids, daughter of John Weare, Esq., of Cedar Rapids.

CHILDREN:

35.   I.   Martha Weare Hubbard, born July 22, 1886, at Chicago; married Sept. 26, 1908, at Lake Forest, Ill., Henry E. Cooke, Jr., born at Philadelphia, son of Rev. Henry E. Cooke and Esther C. Russell; daughter Cynthia Ashley Cooke, born November 1, 1910, at Beverly Farms, Mass.
36.   II. Alice Frances Hubbard, born Jan. 20, 1889, at Chicago; married Sept. 24, 1910, at Lake Forest, Ill., Robert Whitman Means, born May 3, 1886, at Boston, son of Robert Lawrence Means and Jessie M. Whitman. Their daughter, Alice Frances Means, born March 20, 1912, at Beverly Farms, Mass.
37.   III. Eleanor Hubbard, born Sept. 13, 1891, at Chicago.
38.   IV. William Coit Hubbard, born June 11, 1896, at Chicago.

20. HENRY MASCARENE HUBBARD [3] (William C.,[2] Samuel [1]), son of William Coit Hubbard and Alice Frances Hammond, was born February 9, 1860, at Chicago, Illinois; married June 25, 1902, at New York City, Louisa Shipman, born June 20, 1871, at Lexington, Kentucky, daughter of Rev. Jacob S. Shipman of Whitesboro, New York.

CHILDREN:

39. I. Anna Louise Hubbard, born Feb. 24, 1907, at Chicago.

40. II. Alice Coit Hubbard, born March 5, 1911, at Chicago; died May 15, 1912.

21. FLORENCE MASCARENE HUBBARD [3] (James M.,[2] Samuel [1]), daughter of James Mascarene Hubbard and Sarah Hill Tomlinson, was born November 27, 1864, at Boston, Massachusetts; married January 12, 1893, at Longwood, Massachusetts, Robert Rantoul, born June 30, 1862, at Salem, Massachusetts, son of Robert Samuel Rantoul and Harriet C. Neal.

CHILD:

41. I. Florence Mascarene Rantoul, born December, 1893, at St. Paul, Minn.; died January, 1894, at St. Paul.

25. FREDERIC TRACY HUBBARD [3] (Charles E.,[2] Samuel [1]), son of Charles Eustis Hubbard and Caroline Dennie Tracy, was born September 28, 1875, at Boston, Massachusetts; married April 14, 1909, Mary Bessie Welling, born December 30, 1880, at Shediac, New Brunswick, daughter of George W. Welling and Eliza Hall of Shediac.

CHILDREN:

42. I. Charles Eustis Hubbard, born April 6, 1910, at Stoughton, Mass.

43. II. Llewellyn Hall Hubbard, born July 12, 1911, at Manchester, Mass.

27. GERTRUDE HUBBARD [3] (Charles E.,[2] Samuel[1]), daughter of Charles Eustis Hubbard and Caroline Dennie Tracy, was born February 1, 1880, at Boston, Massachusetts; married December 10, 1907, at Boston, Harry Buckle, Captain Royal Field Artillery of England, born in India, died November 12, 1908, at Woolwich, England, son of Harry Buckle and Emma Wheeler.

INDEX

* Names marked with asterisk (*) are to be found in Windeatt chart, page 102.

118

INDEX TO PLACES

121

CPSIA information can be obtained
at www.ICGtesting.com
Printed in the USA
BVHW010949050620
580965BV00010B/124